FOR WHICH IT STANDS

An Anecdotal Biography of the American Flag

MICHAEL CORCORAN

Simon & Schuster

New York   London   Toronto   Sydney   Singapore

SIMON & SCHUSTER
Rockefeller Center
1230 Avenue of the Americas
New York, NY 10020

SIMON & SCHUSTER and colophon are registered trademarks
of Simon & Schuster, Inc.

For information regarding special discounts for bulk purchases,
please contact Simon & Schuster Special Sales:
1-800-456-6798 or business@simonandschuster.com

Book design by Ellen R. Sasahara

Manufactured in the United States of America

1   3   5   7   9   10   8   6   4   2

Library of Congress Cataloging-in-Publication Data

Corcoron, Mike.
For which it stands : an anecdotal biography of the American flag /
Michael Corcoran.
    p.   cm.
Includes bibliographical references and index.
1. Flags—United States—History.   I. Title.
CR113 .C73 2002
929.9'2'0973—dc21   2002029430

ISBN 0-7432-3617-3

ACKNOWLEDGMENTS

The author is indebted to the following people for their gracious gifts of time and interest: Whitney Smith, Ph.D.; Tony Reidy; Amy Munichiello; Harry A. Dooley; Vincent Laurich; Edward Clark, Capt. USN (Ret.); Margaret M. Malone; Timothy Maloney; Carter Beard; Dale Coots; John Dreher; Rod Cantrell; James Corcoran; Kathleen Corcoran; Randall Voorhees; John Monteleone.

I am also grateful to my editor at Simon & Schuster, Jeffrey Neuman, for his faith in me. Also at Simon & Schuster, thanks to Jon Malki for his encouragement and hard work.

For Maryellen, Peter, and Matt

FOR WHICH IT
STANDS

1

T THE END OF 1776, the members of the Continental Congress hotfooted it from Philadelphia to Baltimore, compelled to do so by the uncomfortable proximity of the British armies in New Jersey under General Lord Charles Cornwallis. Six months after they had declared the United States a sovereign nation, there was no shortage of worries for the itinerant Congress. Of primary concern was the ongoing fight to establish independence; most alarming was the dire situation of George Washington's army, which numbered just a few thousand poorly supplied men, many of whom were reaching the end of their one-year enlistment. There was also the matter of devising a set of laws for the new country, a debate begun shortly after the issuing of the Declaration of Independence. By the time the Congress felt safe enough to move back to Philadelphia in March 1777, the Articles of Confederation were still not ratified, and there was another situation that required urgent attention: namely, the attempt to secure foreign aid so that the war could be continued.

On June 14, 1777, in the midst of much more pressing business, the Marine Committee of the Congress scratched out a single sentence that led to the establishment of what would eventually become the world's most recognized symbol: *"Resolved,* That the flag of the thirteen United States be thirteen stripes alternate red and white; that the union be thirteen stars, white in a blue field, representing a new constellation."

The resolution was passed without a shred of romance; angels did not appear over Philadelphia blowing trumpets or singing, nor did Mel Gibson charge into battle a few weeks later carrying the new banner, cutting down the dastardly Redcoats with his avenging sword. Rather, the resolution establishing the flag was passed in the ordinary course of business by the Congress, a single sentence squeezed in among pages of resolutions. Directly preceding the flag resolution came this one: "Resolved, That the marine committee be empowered to give such directions respecting the continental ships of war in the river Delaware as they think proper in case the enemy succeed in their attempts on the said river." Immediately after the flag resolution, the Congress noted that "The council of the state of Massachusetts bay having represented by letter to the president of the Congress that Capt. John Roach sometime since appointed to command the continental ship of war the Ranger is a person of doubtful character and ought not to be entrusted with such a command." Faced with this personnel problem, the Congress resolved to replace Roach with John Paul Jones. (In later years, Jones was fond of telling anyone who would listen that he and the flag were inextricably linked, having been decreed on the same day, as it were.)

The creation of a new national flag had been on the minds of the members of Congress for some time. Marine-supply merchants in Philadelphia had been nagging the governing body about a new flag, so that they could make and sell it. Commanders of both land and naval forces inquired in letters to headquarters about which flag they should use. The need for a standardized flag was obvious, particularly because of the crucial communication and identification purposes banners served in eighteenth century warfare, but not a priority when the survival of the infant republic was in serious jeopardy.

One reason that the Congress didn't act with greater urgency in describing and approving a national flag was that there already *was* an American flag—they just hadn't signed off on it. Since January 2, 1776, a banner known as the Continental Colors had been the *de facto* flag of the nation. The Continental Colors had thirteen stripes; in some cases, the stripes were red and white, but there were often blue stripes, as well. The upper-left corner of the flag (the part the Congress referred to as the "blue field," but primarily known as the *canton*) featured the original British Union Jack, which differed slightly from its modern incarnation. It was this flag that was raised over Prospect Hill, about a mile from Harvard Square in current-day Somerville, Massachusetts, on January 2, 1776, so that the British army in Boston could see it. The Continental Colors was the national flag on July 4, 1776, the day independence was declared. Even some other nations recognized the Continental Colors as the flag of the United States; when the American ship *Andrea Doria* made her way into the Caribbean harbor of St. Eustatius on November 16, 1776, she was flying the Continental Colors. The *Andrea Doria* fired a salute to the Dutch fort on the coast of the island, and the Dutch gunners returned the favor in kind. This was the first recorded acknowledgment of American independence and the new nation's flag.

Still, there was something not quite right about the Continental Colors, and that something was plain to see: the canton consisting of the Union Jack. Its inclusion in the flag's design reflected an early hope that the hostilities between the colonies and Great Britain would not lead to a permanent schism, but its presence was jarring and contradictory as the former colony fought to wrest its independence from the British.

On June 3, 1777, a request was presented to the Congress by a Native American named Thomas Green. In accordance with what by then had become established custom, Green sought the flag of the new nation to present to his tribe. Both the British and the French had established this custom by presenting, among other things, silver, wristbands, money, and flags to various tribes in an attempt to be received favorably by the natives. Green's request, combined with those of the merchants and the military, prompted the Congress to realize the time had come to do something about the flag; after all, having native allies could prove useful in the conduct of the war. At the time of Green's request, any hope of avoiding a total break with the British had long since vanished. Aware of the obvious relationship between the Continental

Colors and the Union Jack, the Congress realized that presenting the flag then in use would be a muddled statement of independence. Thus, the commitment to the Stars and Stripes was made on June 14, 1777.

Content to have removed the issue from its to-do list, the Congress turned back to the business at hand, unaware that they had started a love affair between a people and a flag that would have no equal.

"I DON'T KNOW of the first flag in human civilization," says Whitney Smith, Ph.D., and if Smith doesn't know of it, no one does. Smith, 62, is the world's most ardent devotee of *vexillology,* the study of flags. In fact, Smith coined the term as a 16-year-old high-school student. "I was doing work on the history of flags," says Smith, "and there wasn't any word for it. If you were into coats of arms, you used the word *heraldry.* If you were into coins, it was *numismatics.* So, I used my schoolboy Latin to create the word *vexillology.*" The Latin word for flag is *vexillum,* and Smith added the Greek ending that indicates scholarly study (*-ology*) to form his new word. By 1965, the word began appearing in dictionaries, and it is now a standard entry in both *Webster's* and the *Oxford English Dictionary.*

In the years since he invented his word, Smith has graduated *magna cum laude* from Harvard (1961); founded (1961) and still edits the bimonthly *The Flag Bulletin;* founded (1961) and still directs The Flag Research Center in Winchester, Massachusetts; received a master's degree (1962) and a doctorate (1968) from Boston University; founded the International Federation of Vexillological Associations (1969), which bestowed upon him laureate honors in 1991; authored 22 books on flags and political symbolism, of which more than 300,000 copies have been sold; won the Whitney Award, named after him, from the North American Vexillological Association; and, for good measure, designed the national flag of Guyana while still a student at Harvard. Smith's consultant work over the years has included such clients as the United Nations, the U.S. Department of Defense, NASA, the European Community, IBM, the Olympic Games, the Smithsonian Institution, and the British Museum, among hundreds of others.

Based on his lifelong obsession with flags it would be an easy assumption that Smith is a nerd of the first order. Not so. Even though he jokes that "I didn't have many friends as a kid," he is warm, gracious, and has a brilliant sense of humor. Sitting in his office in Winchester, Smith's effervescence and wit are evident as he talks about flags. "Flags are clearly related to other kinds of symbols," he says. "The Ice Man found in the Alps between Austria and Italy was five thousand years old, and he had tattoos. The Picts in Scotland got their name from the Latin word meaning *with designs.* The name was given to them because they painted their bodies. In both cases, we're looking at a form of body language. These people are saying, 'I'm part of this certain group; possibly they were just saying, 'I am me,' just like people who get tattooed today. It's more likely a case of the former than the latter. That idea of expressing yourself, for whatever reason—to be identifiable in battle; to announce you're part of a community; joy, anger, or sorrow—that's what the development of flags is rooted in. You can see it today in some societies. In third-world countries, where flags aren't readily available, people will take branches and wave them in moments of celebration or victory. Recently, I've started thinking about what primate behavior may have lent itself to the invention of flags—it might be as simple as having something that's an extension of the arm to go along with the beating of the breast and the baring of teeth and so forth to say, 'This is my territory.'

"The process," continues Smith, "of using something to reinforce or take the place of primate display behavior is very ancient. Often, the things didn't take the form of flags as we know them today, but the connection is unmistakable. A staff with an object at the top served the same purpose as a flag. That object might have been carved wood or leather. The Aztecs used feathers, the Mongolians the tail of a tiger. There is in existence today a metal flag with carvings on it from ancient Persia. It's on a staff with an eagle atop it. We don't know much about its antecedents or its use, but it's frighteningly similar to a modern flag. What we do know is that it's 50 centuries old—that's 5,000 years.

"Flags are a serious part of human social organization. In predynastic Egypt, flags flew in front of the temples—there are images of that—and the ancient Egyptian hieroglyphic that represented the gods was a flag. The association is clear: If you wanted to find a god, you went to the temple. If you wanted to find the temple, you looked for the flag."

The use of flags as representations of gods and God caught on; when flags eventually came to be made of cloth, and the wind caught a flag just so, it wasn't too drastic a leap for a person to believe a flag was the living symbol of a deity or a particular saint or a king (many of whom fancied they had a direct connection with or were themselves divine). The feeling that God or king was personally on hand served to comfort a man, particularly when he stood poised to do battle in the name of said God or king, knowing full well he was just minutes away from almost certain death.

FLAGS AS THE cloth banners we know today "almost certainly evolved as part of ancient Chinese sericulture," says Smith. "The silk was light and durable, and it could be painted or embroidered." The Chinese were making silk for nearly 3,000 years before the birth of Christ, but it wasn't until the second century B.C. that traders ambled west along the 4,000-mile Silk Road that led them to the markets of the eastern Mediterranean. From that point, the silk found its way to Rome, and the Romans, busy conquering the western world at the time, may have used silk (or other material) to fashion the *vexilla* carried by the tramping legions. These were usually red, and hung by the top edge from a crosspiece crowning a staff, a method of display perhaps borrowed from the ancient Greeks. The staffs from which the *vexilla* hung were adorned at the top, initially with either a wolf, minotaur, wild boar, horse, or eagle, depending on the military division carrying it; around 100 B.C. the eagle became the primary staff-topping of the legions. In the field, the *vexilla* hung before the general's tent and were used to give the signal to make ready for battle. The Romans used a variety of signaling methods once the collision of forces began: *vocalia* were verbal orders; *semivocalia* were orders given by trumpets; *muta* were signals that made use of the movement of the *vexilla*. The Romans were fond of their eagles and *vexilla;* in some cases, Legion commanders ordered the eagles flung forward into the mass of the enemy in order to inspire their troops. The logic was simple: That eagle is ours, now go and get it.

For some unknown reason, the transition from top-hanging *vexilla* to laterally attached flags that rippled in the wind took eons. Writing in his 1922 book *British Flags,* W. G. Perrin observes: "It is difficult to understand why an invention so apparently simple as the laterally-attached flag should have been so late in making its appearance in Europe (except in the form of small ribbonlike streamers), but the fact remains that it is not until the close of the eighth century A.D. that we meet with evidence of its existence." Perrin goes on to describe a mosaic ordered by Pope Leo III around the year 800. In the mosaic, Christ is handing the keys of the church to Pope Sylvester and a flag to Emperor Constantine; to the left of Christ, St. Peter is offering a cape to Leo (apparently not among the more modest popes) and a flag to Charlemagne, who was crowned emperor of Western Europe on Christmas Day that same year. Both flags in the mosaic are laterally attached to staffs.

Loosely speaking, the seminal moment in the creation of the American flag occurred a few hundred years after laterally flying flags surfaced in Europe. The impetus was the conquering of Jerusalem by the Seljuk Turks in the eleventh century. The Turks did not welcome Christian pilgrims with open arms, which didn't sit well with many Christians in Europe, not the least of whom was Pope Urban II, who believed the Holy Land should be reclaimed from the infidels. Urban II gave his marching orders for the Crusades in 1095, declaring: "God wills it. Christ Himself will be your leader when you fight for Jerusalem." The crusaders packed up their axes, arrows, and swords and traipsed back and forth across the continent for the next 200 years or so.

According to Perrin, something the crusaders most assuredly did not do, despite their alliance under the command of Christ Himself, was march under anything resembling national flags. "If we expect to find traces of any national or popular flags among the early banners carried by the crusaders we shall be disappointed. The kings, nobles, and military orders . . . had each their own special banner, but the common people had none, and it was not until the year 1188, one hundred years after the first crusaders had entered Syria, that a means was provided for distinguishing the rank and file of different nationalities by a variation in the color of the crosses upon their shoulders. From the beginning, the cross set upon the clothing of rich and poor alike had been the outward symbol of a common religion . . . but the flags which led the armies into action and crowned the towers of captured castles or the gates of towns were those of individual leaders."

The crosses sewn to the clothing of the crusaders to differentiate nationality had an impact on later flags. "The Scots used a white diagonal cross," says Smith. "The English used a red cross on white; a white cross on blue was France, a red diagonal on white was Spain, and so forth. They [color-coded crosses] certainly weren't used in the home countries to any great extent. It cannot really be said that these were national symbols and considered as such at the time. But the use of the crosses was important in the process. They were antecedents. The British Union Jack is based on three national crosses, two of which [England and Scotland] are very old." Thousands would die wearing them, but the identifying crosses worn by the Europeans survived the colossal mess of the Crusades.

The stated goal of the Crusades, the liberation of the Holy Land, was not achieved in the end. The motivation of the Crusaders was not always altruistic, and often the traveling warriors lost their bearings and ended up fighting for political purposes or plain old greed. Jerusalem was taken on several occasions, only to be lost again. The first Christian recapturing of the city took place in 1099; however, a key battle along the way took place at Antioch in late 1098. At Antioch, "the city of great towers," the crusaders besieged the Turks for six months. Both sides suffered miserably, and in the final battle there was a noteworthy event: Legend has it that the weary crusaders were moved to victory by the presence of St. George. Shocking indeed, since the good saint had been dead since the third century, but in his battlefield debut he carried the day.

Having earned his stripes at Antioch, St. George was once again dispatched to the front by Christ Himself slightly more than three hundred years later. George's big day came on October 25, 1415, at Agincourt, France. For about sixty-five years prior to that day, St. George was considered the protector of the English crown, which at Agincourt was worn by Henry V. Henry's army of 6,000 or so was on the move toward Calais so their leader could claim the French crown (nothing like the quest for matching crowns to get a good dustup started), and conservative estimates put the number of Frenchmen who met them along the way at 20,000, with some suggestion that there were six times that number. The two forces commenced the battle; the fifteenth-century *Chronicle of England* describes the scene:

> And that day the Frenche men syhe Seint George in the eyre ouer the hoste of the Englisshe men, fyghtyng ayenst the Frenche men; and therfor they worship & holde of Seint George, in Engelond, more than in many other londe . . . and thus Almyhti God & Seint George brought oure enemyes to grounde, & yaf us the victory that day.

The text does not say whether Seint George stayed for refreshments after the fyghtyng ended; but the Englisshe men *and* the Frenche men were certain that they had seen him. (At least according to the legend as it evolved over time; latter-day scholars have suggested that the *Chronicle of England* got its facts mixed up interpreting some poems about Agincourt, and that no one who was actually there ever claimed to have seen St. George. Rather, the poems upon which *Chronicle* based its account indicated the king simply invoked the name of St. George prior to the fight. The legend makes for a much better story, which is why it's legendary.) The following January, the Archbishop of Canterbury proclaimed that the feast day of St. George be considered second in importance only to Christmas and Easter. Henceforth, said the archbishop, George was "the special protector and patron of the English nation." By the end of the 1400s, the red cross of the crusaders had been adopted as the symbol of St. George, and was put to considerable use by various kings. In 1495, Parliament outlawed all battle cries except those which invoked the king and St. George.

Three years before the Act of Parliament regulating English battle cries, Cristoforo Colombo, an Italian explorer leading a small fleet of Spanish vessels searching for a short cut to the Far East, stumbled upon the island of St. Salvador. The Age of Exploration was open for business, and St. George's Cross was on the move to the New World.

IN HIS DEFINITIVE *Origin and History of the American Flag* (1887), George Henry Preble set the mood in the king of England's court following the voyage of Columbus: "There was great talk of the undertaking of Columbus, which was affirmed to be a thing more divine than human, and his fame and report increased in the hearts of some of the king's subjects a great flame of desire to attempt something alike notable." The king at the time was Henry VII, mostly remembered for his eventual victory in the Wars of the Roses and the establishment of the Star Chamber. From an American perspective, however, his primary contribution to the future nation was his deep pockets. In response to the "flame of desire" emanating from his subjects. Henry issued, on March 5, 1496, a patent to Giovanni Caboto to sail "under the royal banners and ensigns, to all parts, countries, and seas, of the east, of the west, and of the north, and to seek out and discover whatsoever they might be, which before this time had been unknown to Christians." If Caboto and his retinue found anything, the patent continued, they should "set up the royal banners and ensigns in the countries, places, or mainland newly found by them." In other words, Henry VII gave his explorers free rein to claim any land for the king, by force if necessary.

Caboto, known to us today as John Cabot, sailed in May 1497, with five ships and his three sons. On the voyage—quite a short one by the standards of the day—they hit upon present-day North America, somewhere around Labrador. The Cabots thought they had found Asia, and claimed to have sailed south along the coast for some time; Preble, a United States Navy admiral, disputes the southerly drift, since the Cabots returned to England three months after leaving (and with just a single ship). A year later, John Cabot and his son Sebastian sailed again. The father died on the journey; the son, however, sailed down the east coast of the future United States, realizing along the way that he wasn't looking at Asia. Wrote Preble: "English flags were the first which were planted along these shores, and Englishmen were the first of the modern Europeans who with their own eyes surveyed the great assemblage of countries in which they were destined to become prominent; and were also the first to put their feet upon it. The history of each one of the chain of states stretching along the western shores of the Atlantic begins with Sebastian Cabot and his expedition in 1498." Strictly speaking, Cabot was not an Englishman, but he was an agent of Henry VII; his crew likely contained some Englishmen.

Little was done to advance exploration of the land Cabot discovered. Henry VII and his son, Henry VIII, sent out other voyages, but the ostensible goal was still to find a shorter route to the Far East. One such voyage in 1536 was a complete calamity and resulted in the death of nearly everyone involved, and this disastrous excursion soured the crown on the notion of dipping into the coffers for another try.

For the next fifty years, no Englishmen or crosses of St. George appeared in America. The dirty work, however, was done; the English knew America was there, and they would return. In the meantime, royal intrigue would continue to shape the flag of the United States. The brouhaha centered around two cousins: Mary Queen of Scots, a Catholic, and Elizabeth, the daughter of the decidedly un-Catholic Henry VIII and Anne Boleyn. To say the cousins disliked each other would be to greatly understate things; their rivalry got serious in 1558, when Elizabeth ascended the throne of England. The Queen of Scots was trouble, something she made clear when she looked the other way at the assassination in 1567 of her second husband, Lord Darnley, at the hands of conspirators led by Lord Bothwell, who subsequently married Mary. The Scots rebelled and threw Mary in jail; she escaped, abdicated her crown, and went to England, where she raised an army to make a nuisance of herself to Elizabeth. Copious amounts of scheming ensued and eventually Elizabeth had Mary imprisoned in 1568. While Mary sat in jail, Elizabeth got busy sponsoring early attempts at colonizing the New World. The settlers called their colony Virginia, in honor of their—allegedly—Virgin Queen. It wasn't until twenty years later, in 1587, that Elizabeth ordered the execution of Mary.

When Mary flew the coop in Scotland, her son by Lord Darnley, James VI, stood next in line for the Scottish crown. James assumed control of Scotland in 1583, and when the Virgin Queen died in 1603, he was the next relative in line for the crown of England. There is no little dark humor in that, upon the death of the woman who ordered his mother's head chopped off, James became the sole king of England and Scotland. In this capacity, he called himself James I.

James I was a rotten king. Seemingly unaware of the destructive nature of religious contention, despite the rift between his mother and her cousin, James occupied himself primarily with asserting his divine rights. He managed to alienate the Puritans among his subjects with his strong High Church beliefs (strongly tilted toward Catholicism), and the Parliament disliked him as well. His unpopular actions didn't stop there: To the chagrin of many, he issued in 1606 a proclamation that combined the flags of England and Scotland into a single design, representative of his united kingdom. The red cross of St. George and its white background were married with the white diagonal cross of St. Andrew's with its blue field. This red, white, and blue blur of crosses was known as the *King's Colors,* and intended solely for use as a naval flag, otherwise known as a *jack.* In 1634, the British historian Rushworth noted that "the union flag, that is the St. George's and St. Andrew's crosses joined together, was still to be reserved as an ornament of power of the king's own ships, and ships in his immediate service and pay, and none other." English ships still flew the red cross and Scottish ships the white, but they occupied a secondary position to the king's union jack.

This 1693 painting (whose authorship is lost to history) depicts just how important a role flags played at sea, announcing the nationality of the ship and its crew. The flag overhanging this ship's bow is the Union Jack, commissioned by King James I and reserved exclusively for royal vessels. St. George's Cross, the foundation of the Union Jack, is also evident among the ship's flags.

Rushworth makes it clear that the King's Colors were the sovereign's alone. They were not intended to, nor did they, represent the people that lived on the island he ruled.

"FOR MILLENNIA," says Whitney Smith, "flags were essentially the right of and restricted to the ruling classes—the priests and the kings who told people how the world worked and why they should be obedient. Flags were used for religious ceremonies, coronations, and on the battlefield, but they were very limited in number. When you get to the Middle Ages, there is an extension through heraldry [coats of arms] to an elite class to personal standards and banners. It was one of the things they were entitled to that ordinary people were not. It is often pointed out that all classes had coats of arms, but this is true only in the sense that, today, there are some poor people who own expensive cars. It was a rarity, and totally different from being among the ruling classes.

"When international shipping grew into something more than hopping from one port to the next, flags were used for signaling purposes. The great fleets of the 1700s and 1800s—and even much earlier—made extensive use of them. The sailors had to know friend from enemy, and a ship without a flag was considered a pirate. Pirates, of course, sometimes used flags as a ruse to get people within their grasp. By the end of the seventeenth century, flags were being used to such an extent that a guide book to flags appears in 1695. The book was necessary because flying the wrong flag—or failing to properly identify one—could land you in big trouble. On the other hand, there was no emotional attachment to most of them, and there was no extensive use of them on land. It's not as if people looked to them as being *their* flag. For that feeling to evolve, you have to look to the democratic countries, where the citizens became involved as individuals and not just as part of the masses or as soldiers.

"One of the first flags to take on the feeling of a national flag was the original Dutch tricolor of orange, white, and blue. During the Dutch uprising in the Netherlands—the Eighty Years War, which started in the mid-sixteenth century and lasted until 1648—people used the flag in local communities. It showed their allegiance to Prince William of Orange. They were a seafaring people, so the distinction between land and sea wasn't as sharp as it was in France, for instance, which had coastal communities but primarily had an inland population.

"In the modern sense," continues Smith, "the Continental Colors was the first national flag in the world. It preceded the French Tricolor and, although the Union Jack was around, it was not considered a national flag. It was a royal banner that was used for specific purposes. There were some flags that are used today as national flags, but they weren't used as national flags prior [to the Continental Colors]. The Danish flag, for instance, was a religious flag, a royal flag, and a military flag, but it wasn't until 1848 during a war with Prussia that it became the national flag. The fact that they adopted a flag that was already in existence doesn't mean it was national from the time it was first used.

"The American Revolution and French Revolution are terribly important in the establishment of national flags as we know them today. For the first time, the *people* are saying,

'This is what we stand for. This is what we're fighting for. We're going to make our *own* flags and use them.' "

On January 16, 1707, Parliament officially adopted the King's Colors—the union jack of James I—as the "ensigns armorial to our kingdom . . . to be used on all flags, banners, standards and ensigns both at sea and land." These words were part of the Act of Union, which officially created the united kingdom of Great Britain under Queen Anne. (The modern day Union Jack also includes the red cross of St. Patrick for Ireland, not added to the flag until 1801.)

By the time of the rule of Queen Anne, the American colonies had blossomed, due in large part to the English Puritans who fled for the Massachusetts Bay colony to escape religious persecution during the reign of James I. Two Dutch travelers, Jasper Dankers and Peter Sluyter, recorded their impressions of the New England colonies in 1680:

> New England is now described as extending from the Fresh [Connecticut] River to Cape Cod and thence to Kennebec [Maine], comprising three provinces or colonies—Fresh River, or Connecticut, Rhode Island and the other islands to Cape Cod, and Boston, which stretches from thence north. They are subject to no one, but acknowledge the king of England for their lord, and therefore no ships enter unless they have English passports or commissions . . . Each province chooses its own governor from the magistracy, and the magistrates are chosen from the principal inhabitants, merchants or planters. They are all independent in matters of religion, if it can be

called religion; many of them perhaps more for the purpose of enjoying the benefits of its privileges than for any regard to truth and godliness. I observed that while the English flag or color has a red ground with a small white field in the uppermost corner where there is a red cross [St. George's], they have dispensed with this cross in their color and preserved the rest.

(As will be seen, the crossless flag described was what remained when the St. George's cross was literally slashed out of the English flag in 1634 in Salem, Massachusetts, in what may be thought of as the first example of flag desecration in America.)

The independent nature of the New England colonists had been on display for all to see for nearly thirty years before the preceding words were written. A mint was established in Massachusetts in 1652 and the coins it issued clearly point to the twin (and often contradictory) American beliefs of self-determination and unity. On one side of the coins was the word "Massachusetts" and the favored symbol of New England, the pine tree; on the flip side were the words "New England," and the year, 1652 A.D. That year was stamped on every pine tree coin minted for the next thirty years. During that interval, Charles II was placed on the throne by Parliament in 1660, restoring the monarchy that had been interrupted during the English Civil War and Oliver Cromwell's stint as Lord Protector. Charles had every reason to be unaware of goings on in the colonies at the time; he had tried to grab the crown by force in 1651 and was defeated by Cromwell, who had his men search high and low for the upstart Charles. At one point, Charles was concealed in an oak tree to avoid capture. Once he was king, Charles became furious when he learned the Massachusetts colonists had assumed the right to coin money, something only *he* could empower them to do. When shown the coins, Charles II immediately inquired as to the type of tree represented on the coin. Since the quality of the minting process made the image murky, the king was told, "That is the royal oak which saved your majesty's life." The speaker, Sir Charles Temple, was a man who looked favorably upon the colony, and his little white lie assuaged the king's tantrum. Hoodwinked into believing the colonists had given him his just due by using the royal oak, Charles called them "a parcel of honest dogs."

Charles's cheeky reference to the colonists as dogs was surely harmless, and it's easy to imagine him tittering as he said it. The New England colonists, however, might have taken umbrage had they heard the remark. The increasing weariness they felt at being beholden to the crown wouldn't boil over for another hundred years and, even then, there was some initial hesitancy about severing ties with the monarchy. However, the national identity of the United States was beginning to take form, and the colonists would rely more and more on flags as a means of letting the British know how they felt. One of the earliest among such flags was the pine tree banner of New England.

THE CONTINENTAL COLORS were raised over the Cambridge camp at Prospect Hill on January 2, 1776, to celebrate the official forming of the Continental Army and to show the British there was still some fight left in the colonials, despite the thrashing they had taken on Breed's Hill in June of 1775. The battle on the hill in Charlestown was the first major bloodletting of the revolution; both sides were battered, and retired—the colonials beat a retreat to Cambridge and the British headed to Boston to put their feet up awhile. It cannot be said with any certainty which flags, if any, flew over the colonial ranks during the battle (which has gone down mistakenly in history as the Battle of Bunker Hill). The most famous painting of the battle, by John Trumbull (who watched the fight through a spyglass from a distance of about four miles) shows the colonials engaged in hand-to-hand combat under a Pine Tree flag—a red field with a white canton containing a pine tree—and two other flags, one of solid red and another, only partially visible in the rendering, that is difficult to discern. Trumbull, a brilliant artist, admitted later that he couldn't really see what was going on through the spyglass, and he is known to have fudged details in his work—particularly those pertaining to flags—for dramatic effect. Certainly, he wasn't the first, nor the last, artist to make use of that profession's well-known license.

The Pine Tree flag may well have hovered over the bayonets on Breed's Hill. Who's to say? There were many flag designs in use in the colonies at the time. Some of the most popular were flags featuring a rattlesnake, often combined with the words "Don't Tread On Me," which remain etched in the American mind even today because of the sentiment they express: Namely, we're tough customers when the situation calls for it.

The rattlesnake was used symbolically in the colonies for

John Trumbull's 1786 painting, *The Death of General Warren at the Battle of Bunker's Hill, June 17, 1775.* Note that the flag flying in the upper left-hand corner has a pine tree in its canton.

the first time in 1754 as a result of the Albany Congress. That gathering, which lasted from June 19 to July 11, included delegates from the colonies of New York, Pennsylvania, New Hampshire, Connecticut, Massachusetts, Rhode Island, and Maryland; among the delegates from Pennsylvania was Benjamin Franklin. The group assembled, along with 150 representatives of the Iroquois Indian Federation, at the behest of the London Board of Trade, to discuss two main topics: issues the Iroquois had with the colonies and the increasingly hostile French forces who, allied with other Indian tribes, presented clear and present danger to the colonies.

The result of the Albany Congress was a plan written by Franklin, which called for one main colonial body to deal with Indian affairs, laws, and taxes, with the presiding officer appointed by the king. However, the plan never took effect, primarily because both sides—the colonies and the king—felt it granted the other too much power. Franklin's plan had plenty of merit, and parts of it inspired sections of the Declaration of Independence more than twenty years later. Before the Albany plan went down in flames, Franklin stumped for its adoption by creating a cartoon that showed a rattlesnake separated into segments representing the various colonies. The image was captioned simply: "Unite or Die."

"Many people today think that was a flag," says Whitney Smith, "and they look for reproductions of what they refer to as the 'Join or Die' flag. There never was one. It was a cartoon, but it had a tremendous influence on later flags. The snake as a symbol was used extensively prior to that time. It had antecedents in Europe, where a snake biting its own tail was a symbol of eternity. Rattlesnakes appealed to colonials because the snakes were indigenous to America, and didn't strike unless provoked. Even then, before they struck, they gave warning, but when their patience was at an end, look out!" It was common at the time to believe that the timber rattlesnake, the model for the later flags, had thirteen rattles. In fact, the number of rattles varies from snake to snake.

Twenty years after the Albany Congress, Franklin's cartoon popped up again, during the flap that ensued after the passing of the Stamp Act by Parliament. On November 17, 1774, the newspaper *Massachusetts Sun* ran the snake cartoon under its banner, and over a story encouraging the people of Quebec to join the resistance to the king. In short order, images of snakes were as plentiful in the colonies as the snakes themselves.

The rattlesnake eventually appeared on two flags still recognizable today: One, known as the Gadsden Flag, is a yellow banner with a white rattlesnake coiled over the words "Don't Tread on Me." It is believed that Christopher Gadsden, a member of the Continental Congress from South Carolina, created this flag to present to the provincial assembly of his home colony. Gadsden's inspiration was provided by the rank flag of Commodore Esek Hopkins, the first commander-in-chief of the Continental Navy; the commodore's flag, flown from the main mast, featured the rattlesnake extended diagonally across a background of red and white stripes, with its head near the upper left. Today, Hopkins' rank flag is referred to as the first navy jack. "The flag flown by Commodore Hopkins really struck a chord with people, as did the 'Don't Tread on Me' motto," says Smith.

"Versions of those flags have been used ever since, including by the Confederacy in the Civil War."

Of all the rattlesnake flags, however, the one that displayed the most direct feeling of the gathering storm of independence was that of the Proctor's Independent Battalion, Westmoreland County, Pennsylvania. John Proctor's men first raised the flag in 1775. Proctor's gang did not fight in the Revolution as a unit, and so, it is unknown if the flag ever saw battle. It was fashioned from an old British ensign of solid red with a small Union Jack in the corner. The person who reworked the flag for Proctor placed a coiled rattlesnake with thirteen rattles over the words "Don't Tread on Me," and the head of the snake was quite purposefully striking at the Union Jack.

Nonetheless, despite the popularity and resonance of the rattlesnake flags, when the New Year rolled in and a flag appeared over Prospect Hill thumbing the colonial nose at the British, it was the Continental Colors—thirteen red and white stripes, with the Union Jack of the day in the canton. The flag may have been used weeks previous on a ship or two, but its big unveiling was ordered by Washington at Prospect Hill (though it's unclear if the general was there in person). Interestingly enough, the flag raising coincided with the arrival in the colonies of a letter from George III, in which he averred that all would be forgiven if the colonials would just admit the error of their ways.

There or not, we do have Washington's impressions of the moment from a letter he wrote on January 4: "We are at length favored with the sight of his Majesty's most gracious speech, breathing sentiments of tenderness and compassion for his deluded American subjects . . . and farcical enough, we gave great joy to them [the British in Boston] without knowing or intending it, for on that day which gave being to our new army, but before the [king's] proclamation came to hand, we hoisted the union flag in compliment to the United Colonies. But, behold! It was received at Boston as a token of the deep impression the speech had made upon us, and as a signal of submission.

"By this time [the writing of the letter], I presume they begin to think it strange that we have not made a formal surrender of our lines."

There was *some* confusion regarding the new flag. Preble cites an anonymous letter written on January 2 that reads in part: "The grand union flag of thirteen stripes was raised on a height near Boston. The regulars [British soldiers] did not understand it; and as the king's speech had just been read, as they supposed, they thought the *new* flag was a token of submission."

Not all who witnessed the event were so misled. A British transport captain wrote from Boston to the ship's owners in London on January 17: "I can see the rebels' camp very plain, whose colors a little while ago, were entirely red; but on the receipt of the king's speech, which they burnt, they hoisted the union flag, which is here supposed to intimate the union of the provinces."

In London, the *Annual Register* reported similarly: "They burnt the king's speech, and changed their colors from a plain red ground, which they had hitherto used, to a flag with thirteen stripes, as a symbol of the union and number of the

The Continental Colors were raised above Prospect Hill on the order of George Washington and became the unofficial flag of the nascent United States.

colonies." (The solid red flags the British correspondents mention were the colors of one or two Connecticut regiments in the rebel camp.)

Because of the references by many, including Washington, to the new flag as a "union flag," the banner raised over Prospect Hill was in later years (and to a large degree to this day) called the Grand Union flag. It was indeed a union flag in the generic sense of those words. The colonials were familiar with the notion of flags showing unity from the frequent sight of the Union Jack and from their own pine-tree and rattlesnake flags. The description of the flag as a "grand union" simply meant that it was a great or large union. There *is* among the many versions of the Stars and Stripes throughout American history one known as the Grand Union, but it would come many years after the revolution. "At the time," says Whitney Smith, "the term continental meant what we mean today by federal. And the word colors meant flag. That flag on Prospect Hill was the Continental Colors, and that's how it was referred to at the time."

The Continental Colors saw extensive use during the next two years. After slight initial confusion among those who first saw it, the British came to understand the message the flag was sending. The key to its significance lay not only in the number of the stripes, but in their color. The red and white stripes were familiar to some of the British onlookers; they were the symbol of the Sons of Liberty, the New England radicals who kick-started the revolution.

2

*T*here is the national flag! He must be cold indeed, who can look upon its folds rippling in the breeze without pride of country. If he be in a foreign land, the flag is companionship, and country itself, with all its endearments. Who, as he sees it, can think of a State merely? Whose eye, once fastened upon its radiant trophies, can fail to recognize the image of the whole nation? It has been called a floating piece of poetry; and yet I know not if it have any intrinsic beauty beyond other ensigns. Its highest beauty is in what it symbolizes. It is because it represents all, that all gaze at it with delight and reverence. It is a piece of bunting lifted in the air; but it speaks sublimely and every part has a voice. It's stripes of alternate red and white proclaim the original union of thirteen States to maintain the Declaration of Independence. Its stars, white on a field of blue, proclaim that union of states constituting our national constellation, which receives a new star with every new state. The two together signify union, past and present. The very colors have a language which was officially recognized by our fathers. White is for purity; red, for valor; blue, for justice. . . .

—CHARLES SUMNER, famed orator and United States senator from Massachusetts, 1852–1874

CHARLES SUMNER is largely forgotten today, except for those who recall that he was savagely beaten by Preston Brooks, a congressman from South Carolina, on the floor of the Senate in 1856. (It was a criminal assault right out of a script from professional wrestling. Brooks used a cane instead of a metal chair, however. It took Sumner three years to physically recover enough to return to public life.) In his day, particularly during the Civil War, Sumner's impassioned oratory made him one of the most famous men in America. This is mentioned here because even Sumner—a Harvard graduate, a lawyer, and a senator—was confused about the origin and significance of the colors red, white, and blue in the American flag, at least if the preceding excerpt from one of his speeches accurately reflects his beliefs.

It's understandable that the honorable senator might have been mistaken about the colors. As time passed from the original flag resolution in 1777, and the flag became more ingrained in everyday American life, a kind of collective mythology and assumed significance were attached to the banner and became part of pop-culture belief.

The design that is popularly thought of as the first American flag—and was indeed the first official Stars and Stripes—is familiar to all Americans: thirteen white stars in a circle upon a blue canton, with thirteen red and white stripes arranged alternately, a red one at the top and a red one at the bottom. Modern-day flag manufacturers call this the Betsy Ross flag in their catalogues and, with the exception of the current fifty-star flag, more of it are sold than any other American flag design. (Incidentally, a Betsy Ross flag is *still* an official American flag, as are each of the other twenty-six official designs of the Stars and Stripes which preceded the current version of fifty stars. Once an official American flag, always an official American flag.)

Attentive readers will have noticed that the original specifications called for in 1777 were far from precise: No mention is made of the meaning of the colors; no direction is given for the shape of the stars, or for their arrangement on the blue canton; the stripes are not described as horizontal, nor does it say to use seven red and six white. This ambiguity raises two questions: What did each element of the flag signify? And how did the final arrangement of these elements come to be?

Many of the answers center around Francis Hopkinson, one of the delegates from New Jersey to sign the Declaration of Independence: Hopkinson was a member of the Marine Committee, as well as one of its subcommittees, known as the Continental Navy Board. His service on the board put him in position to be acutely aware of the need for a common official flag; even though flags were being used on land by the army, they were considered much more vital for navies. On land, it was possible to tell with some accuracy who the antagonists were even without the presence of flags. The same was not true on the vast, open waters. It was, using his own word, Hopkinson's "fancy" to design seals and symbols and the like; in other words, it was his hobby, and he was very good at it. Among his designs were the seals of New Jersey, the U.S. Navy, and the Treasury Department. While a member of the Marine Committee, he started thinking about designs for a unique American flag that would erase any ambiguity created by the Continental Colors.

"Francis Hopkinson designed the flag," says Whitney Smith, "that's very clear from contemporary claims and the lack of contemporary challenges. Here's my theory: Hopkinson realized using the Union Jack was no longer appropriate—there was a lot of talk about it. He may have gone to Congress and said, 'Here's my proposal; we'll keep the red and white stripes because they were used by the Sons of Liberty and they were the ones who got the revolution started. The red and white stripes alone won't do, so let's put in another symbol—a unique one. This is *really* a new country. Every other one has existed for a long time—China, Persia, India—even if it doesn't exist as a unified country today, and even if there isn't a unified central government, it's been around forever. We're *new*. There's never been a United States before. We're the only place in the whole New World with our own government. It's like going out at night and looking up into the sky and seeing an entirely new constellation that wasn't there the night before. So let's use that as our symbol.'" Hopkinson was well acquainted with heraldry, where stars were sometimes used. His own coat of arms, known from its appearances in the books of his personal library, had stars in it (though they were six-pointed), and stars were being used on money at the time.

The brevity of the resolution on June 14, 1777 was not a case of the lawmakers being willfully vague or careless. Rather, Congress felt it didn't need to waste words; they *knew* what the new flag looked like because they were familiar with the design proposed by Hopkinson.

How the flag eventually ended up with five-pointed stars is more of a mystery than the use of stars in general. "Stars were not a common heraldic symbol," says Smith. "They did not appear on any national flag in 1777. There was one city, Norden, in Germany, whose ships used stars on their flag. The stars in heraldry are multipointed, because when you look at a star you don't see five nice little points, you see brilliance. So a multipointed star would more closely resemble what is seen in the heavens. I can't say it's an absolute, but at the time five-pointed stars were basically unknown. As a heraldist, Hopkinson may well have intended for a multipoint star to be used, especially if he was thinking of a formal standard of which there would be only one for marching into Congress and keeping on display there."

The formal standards in the halls of the world's governing bodies at the time were often painted on silk. Multipointed stars could have been painted on such a banner for use in the Continental Congress, for example, but it would have taken great time and care. To make flags in quantity, it was faster to sew the stars on; sewn stars would also be more durable when exposed to the elements, especially at sea. Someone who was handy with a needle could probably sew a flag in a single day. It was more than likely, then, that the practical necessities of sewing led to the use of the five-pointed star. "Hopkinson was not a flag maker," says Smith. "What probably happened was Hopkinson designed the flag, and others start *making* the flag—Betsy Ross among them. Trying to cut the loose weave of the fabric in many points would have been difficult. The people making the flags very quickly go to a five-pointed star because it's easier in general to make, and it's easier to make large so it can be seen. There was no existing model for it, nor would there have been any reason for someone to say, 'The five-pointed star better represents what we mean to say.' "

The stars representing the "new constellation" were to be placed upon a blue canton. So, the first official flag would be comprised of three colors: red, white, and blue. Those three colors have taken on a world of meaning over the subsequent two centuries: Sumner told his listeners that they stood for purity, valor, and justice, and in some songs about the flag, blue is said to stand for loyalty. When the Congress adopted the Great Seal of the United States in 1782, Charles Thomson, the secretary of Congress, submitted "remarks and explanations" for the new seal, including the following:

> The colours of the pales are those used in the flag of the United States of America; White signifies purity and innocence, Red, hardiness & valor, and Blue, the colour of the Chief, signifies vigilance, perseverance and justice. . . .

Thomson's assignment of meaning to the colors red, white, and blue in the Great Seal *vis à vis* the flag was believable enough, but off the mark. More to the point, it was fiction. "People want meaning," says Smith. "And traditionally speaking, it usually comes *ex post facto*. Today, everything is thought out ahead of time. In the past, people weren't afraid to symbolize something with an arbitrary symbol. They knew in time it would come to stand for something. We're afraid to do that today. So, the colors of our flag were only indirectly defined by the proposal for the Great Seal. That's as close as we come. You could argue that the colors mean those things in the Great Seal and the two [flag and seal] are similar. And the Great Seal came early, but it's five years after the flag. Any meaning to the colors of the flag was assigned after the fact, and it's never been officially recognized [that the flag's colors have any meaning]."

In a hairsplitting defense of the long-dead Thomson, it should be noted that he didn't actually *say* that the colors had meaning in the flag; he said the colors in the Great Seal *were the same as those of the flag,* and then went on to define the colors as used in the seal. The connection *seems* implicit in his words, and has been construed as such by generations of Americans.

In truth, there are two reasons the United States ended up with a red, white, and blue flag: familiarity and availability. "I think we can fairly say," says Smith, "that the red, white, and blue were used because they were familiar colors from the Union Jack and the Continental Colors. In heraldry, there were only the basic colors of red, blue, green, and black. There was also yellow, gold, silver, and white, but they were used mostly to separate the other colors. So you typically had either white or gold in your flag in heraldry [as a separator], and it made sense. There weren't any good green dyes in those days—anything green looked muddy. There were two shades of blue—light blue and dark blue. Dark blue was more visible and it held up better. The symbolism of black was negative, and yellow was the color of quarantine, not to mention the use of a yellow flag by Hieronymus Bosch on *The Ship of Fools.* So, there just weren't many choices. And since red, white, and blue were the British colors, it made sense."

The arrangement of the Continental Colors set a precedent that was followed in the first Stars and Stripes: it had two symbols of union—one in the canton (the Union Jack) and the stripes. In the new design, the group of stars was put in the place previously occupied by the Union Jack: The dual expressions of unity didn't leave much doubt as to the new flag's primary symbolism. Hopkinson's arrangement of the stars in a circle likely had several meanings, any or all of which may have been among the following: A constellation of stars does not consist solely of a row of stars; parts of constellations, such as the three stars that form the belt of Orion, appear as rows, but a constellation as a whole is never a straight line. Nor, for that matter, do constellations appear as perfect circles, but a circle more closely resembles a constellation than a straight line; a ring of stars showed unity and equality—no one star is greater than the others; finally, a ring of stars symbolizes eternity, since it has no identifiable starting place or end. (Whitney Smith found two rings of stars—one of nine and one of thirteen—in a seventeenth-century heraldry book. Smith suggests that Hopkinson may have been familiar with these, but is careful to note that the heraldic ring of thirteen—called an Augustan wreath—wouldn't have meant much in the American sense.)

Since the stripes were a foregone conclusion for the most part, it's interesting to consider what might have appeared on the flag in place of the Union Jack if Hopkinson hadn't suggested a ring of stars. Preble devoted some thought to the matter: ". . . What could be found to replace the crosses emblematic of the . . . authority they had renounced? The rattlesnake, which had been used for a time as a symbol of the necessity of the union and defiance . . . was repulsive to many, from being akin to the tempter of our first parents, and the cause of their expulsion from Paradise, bearing also the curse of the Almighty." Another revolutionary symbol known in use around 1776 was a circle of thirteen mailed (armored) hands, clutching the links of an endless chain; in the same vein, a mailed hand clutching thirteen arrows was used on some ships, but that, says Preble, "was a symbol of war and defiance rather than of union." The Philadelphia Light Horse used a round rope knot with thirteen floating ends in its colors. Preble thought this was a "beautiful device, signifying strength in union." What about a checkerboard pattern of white, blue, and red squares? Sounds funky, but Preble points out the odd number made it impossible to use little squares to form one big square. "Thirteen terrestrial objects, such as eagles, bears, trees, would have been absurd," writes Preble (and a checkerboard wouldn't have?) "and equally so would have been thirteen suns or moons; besides, the crescent was the chosen emblem of Mohammedanism [Islam], and therefore unfitted to represent a Christian people. Thirteen crosses would have shocked the sentiments of a portion of the people, who looked upon the cross as an emblem of popish idolatry. There remained only the stars . . ."

The number of red stripes is one greater than the total of white stripes in the flag, which is purely an effect of dealing with an odd number. There is no significance in the fact that a red stripe occupies the top and bottom positions in the union of stripes; it just looked better that way. In modern graphic design parlance, red at the top and bottom framed the entire flag in a more esthetically pleasing manner.

If the members of the Continental Congress could have employed modern communication technology to spread the word regarding the new flag, most of the flags that appeared in the wake of the resolution would have been nearly exact copies of Hopkinson's design. As it was, and with flag production at the time being strictly a cottage industry, flags featuring thirteen stripes and thirteen stars began appearing with the components arranged in every which way. It mattered little: As long as there were thirteen stars and thirteen stripes, it wasn't long before anyone who saw the flag knew it was the national standard of the United States of America. "The thirteen star and thirteen stripe flag was used by common citizens on land as well as at sea," says Smith. "This was contrary to the practice of other countries, which considered every flag to be a symbol of the governing classes."

For his part, Hopkinson was never paid for his design of the flag, even though he lobbied Congress for payment in the ensuing years. They refused to pay him, but they never denied he created the flag.

• • •

ASK ANY AMERICAN CITIZEN who made the first American flag and the answer will almost assuredly be, "Betsy Ross." (This assumes the American citizen you ask is not Whitney Smith, Ph.D.) An equally firm answer will be given if you ask the same person what Francis Hopkinson is most famous for: "I don't know."

No person in American history is more synonymous with the American flag than Betsy Ross, and that she is reflects a well-known facet of the American character: We're suckers for a good patriotic story. In the case of Mrs. Ross, we bit hook, line, and sinker on a whopper.

Her coming out as the queen of American lore occurred nearly a century after the Stars and Stripes were first acknowledged by Congress. In 1870, her grandson, William Canby, addressed the Historical Society of Pennsylvania. Canby asserted in the speech that his grandmother had sewn the very first Stars and Stripes ever made, and that she had contributed to its design. Up until that time, no living American, save for her descendants, had ever heard the tale of Elizabeth Ross and the first flag.

Canby's story proceeded along these lines: In June 1776, a committee of Congress, accompanied by George Washington himself, appeared on the doorstep of Mrs. Ross's home, a rented house on Arch Street in Philadelphia out of which she did upholstering and the like. The group produced a sketch of a flag; she suggested to the general that he draw the flag as he would like to see it, while seated in her parlor. They asked if Betsy could make the flag shown on the adjusted sketch. "I don't know whether I can, but I'll try," she said. She immediately informed them that the six-pointed stars were too difficult to make, but that a five-pointed star could easily be fashioned. The gentlemen agreed. Betsy Ross sewed the flag, and it was blowing in the wind within a matter of days, just in time for the Declaration of Independence!

One of the interesting twists to the story is that Betsy Ross was married three times: her first husband, John Ross (the nephew of Col. George Ross, who was one of the alleged congressional visitors to her house and a signer of the Declaration of Independence), was killed in combat during the revolution; her second husband, a man named Ashburn, died as a prisoner of war in England; her third husband, John Claypole, was a lineal descendent of Oliver Cromwell, the old Lord Protector. Betsy's marital life is crucial to the popularity of her legend. First, she showed old-fashioned gumption when asked to make the flag, at first demurring, and then saying, "but I'll try." That's the American spirit! On top of that, here was a woman left a widow not once, but twice, when her husbands died in the struggle for freedom. Huzza! Who could resist embracing this most patriotic of stories. Besides, Betsy Ross was a Quaker—she wouldn't lie!

Soon after Canby's story got out, there were doubters. He defended his story in a letter cited by George Henry Preble in *Origin and History of the American Flag*, just two years after the 1870 speech:

> It is not *tradition,* it is *report* from the lips of the principal participator in the transaction (Betsy Ross), directly told not to one or two, but a dozen or more living witnesses, of whom I myself am one, though but a little boy when I heard it. I . . . well remember

her telling the story. My mother and two of her sisters are living and in good memory. I have the narrative from the lips of the oldest one of my aunts, now deceased, reduced to writing in 1857. This aunt, Mrs. Clarissa Wilson, succeeded to the business, and continued making flags for the navy yard and arsenals . . . Washington was a frequent visitor at my grandmother's house before receiving command of the army. She embroidered his shirt ruffles, and did many other things for him. He knew her skill with the needle. Colonel Ross, with Robert Morris and General Washington called upon Mrs. Ross, and told her they were a committee of Congress . . . This was prior to the Declaration of Independence. I fix the date to be during Washington's visit to Congress from New York in June, 1776, when he came to confer upon the affairs of the army, the flag being, no doubt, one of these affairs.

Preble wasn't buying Canby's claim, nor have vexillologists in the years since Preble first wrote his book. The speech made by Canby in 1870 was the first public knowledge of the Betsy Ross story. The original speech is in the Huntington Library in San Marino, California. Whitney Smith has read it. "If you read the whole speech," says Smith, "you shudder at the level of his [Canby's] sophistication in dealing with it. The Betsy Ross part is about one-fifth of the total speech. The rest of it contains stuff that is known to be not true."

Canby's presumption that the fateful meeting took place in the spring of 1776 doesn't hold water. "The flag resolution wasn't passed until June 1777," says Smith. "Canby claimed the flag was immediately made by Betsy, taken to a ship in the harbor, hoisted, the people loved it, and Congress adopted it. Fourteen months is not immediate. You can't have it both ways—that Congress adopted it immediately and they did so while Washington was in Philadelphia."

That the meeting in Betsy's house ever took place is highly unlikely. "Washington was not a member of Congress," says Smith. "You don't put a nonmember on a congressional committee. He was the commander-in-chief of the army—he had to go to Congress to ask for money, and get authority for various things. Like any good politician, he had to be careful of how much credibility he had. He wouldn't get involved in details that are Congress's because he needed their support on important things. Designing the flag, making the flag—those are minor details. Colors [regimental, *et al*] for his troops to carry in the field are a different story. We also have to remember the class distinctions of the time; it is not likely that a gentleman farmer—one of the American aristocracy from Virginia—would have gone to a common upholsterer to discuss the making of a flag. Congress wouldn't even send a committee. The story of the meeting at her house strains the overall credibility of the story."

Canby supported his assertion that the Stars and Stripes were in use shortly after the signing of the Declaration of Independence with statements made by the daughter of Captain Hugh Montgomery, commander of the brig *Nancy*. In March 1776, the *Nancy* made its way to Puerto Rico and, eventually, to St. Thomas. There, said the captain's daughter, information was received that independence had been proclaimed, complete with a description of the flag of the new nation. The ship's men gathered together the material and made a Betsy Ross flag, and flew it on the return home. Preble refuted this with certainty: The *Nancy*, he knew as an admiral and naval historian, was blown out of the water on June 29, 1776, before the signing of the Declaration of Independence and, more to the point, well before Betsy Ross's alleged design could have reached the *Nancy* in St. Thomas without the aid of a fax machine.

Staunch Betsyites over the years have pointed to cash receipts that show Ross made flags around the time in question. There is no doubt that Betsy Ross made flags, but any flags she was making in June 1776 were for the navy of Pennsylvania. Among other disparities in the legend: When Betsy's design was approved by Congress, she was asked to make as many flags as possible. She avers she has no money to purchase material. Col. Ross, the story goes, apologizes for his lack of consideration and hands her £100. By today's standards, the colonel had quite a wad of walking-around money in his pocket. He would have been a good guy to bump into at Ye Olde Ale House.

Despite it all, the legend of Betsy Ross remains one that is held dear by Americans. She was not mythical and she did make flags; it is quite possible she made American flags, even those with thirteen stars in a ring, but she did not design the flag. There is no evidence that points to anyone as being the person who actually sewed the first Stars and Stripes, or if the stars were in fact sewn on the first flag, no matter who made it.

No one has ever suggested that Canby lied, or that his

aunts or grandmother lied to him. "The story as presented is just not credible," says Smith. "There are too few details, and the ones we have are doubtful." Smith's take on the legend is that it was a simple misunderstanding: An eleven-year-old kid, Canby, hears his grandmother telling stories about how she used to sit next to George Washington in Christ's Church. *My grandmother knew George Washington!* Betsy's daughters carry on her sewing business [a fact], and while they are sitting around working with the grandson sitting nearby, Betsy regales them with tales of the olden days—the Revolution! During the chat, she says, "I made the first flag." She doesn't mean she made *the* first flag; rather, she says it in the teasing tone a veteran ballplayer uses with a rookie: "Look at these new-fangled flags you're making with their rows of stars and whatnot. When I was in my prime, I made the first flag, the one with thirteen stars." *My grandmother made the first flag!*

"You have to remember when Betsy Ross first arose in America's consciousness," says Smith. "The Civil War was just ended. The country was together again. The Transcontinental Railroad has gone through. The West has opened up, and Manifest Destiny—what God has promised us as a leader of men—is back on track. The centennial of the nation was coming up and there was a big celebration planned in Philadelphia. Everybody is looking for a way to say, 'We're just as good as Europe, and we have the army to prove it.' And so the story comes out in 1870 and there's no alternative to it, and it quickly becomes immensely popular."

If there is anything remarkable about Betsy Ross, it is this: In a war that lasted from 1775 to 1783 and claimed just

4,435 American lives on the battlefield, she lost two husbands. That alone makes her worth remembering.

ASIDE FROM THE CITIZENS of the new nation, the observers with the most curiosity about the new American symbol were the British. The flag was meant to tell the world that the king no longer held sway over the colonies. That being the case, the British were certainly interested in the banner proclaiming their irrelevance. One British historian, named Lowes, was convinced that the stars in the flag were lifted directly from the coat of arms of George Washington's family. The strength of Lowes's conviction in this matter is very British in its nineteenth century belief that a sovereign individual should be at the center of a country and its symbols.

> Like Oliver Cromwell, the American patriot was fond of genealogy, and corresponded with our heralds on the subject of his own pedigree. Yes! that George Washington, who gave sanction if not birth to that most democratical of all sentiments, "that all men are free and equal," was, as the phrase goes, a gentleman of blood, of ancient time, and coat-armor, nor was he slow to acknowledge the fact. When the Americans, in their most righteous revolt against the tyranny of the mother country, cast about for an ensign with which to distinguish themselves from their English oppressors, what did they ultimately adopt? Why! Nothing more nor less than a gentleman's badge, a modification of the old English coat of arms borne by their leader and

deliverer. A few stars had, in the old chivalrous times, distinguished his ancestors from their compeers in the tournament and upon the battle-field; more stars and additional stripes, denoting the number of States that joined in the struggle, now became the standard around which the patriots of the West so successfully rallied. It is not a little curious that the poor worn-out ray of feudalism, as so many would count it, should have expanded into the bright and ample banner that now waves from every sea.

Lowes's theory is the purest form of balderdash. We know so from a letter written by Washington himself to Sir Isaac Heard in 1792. Heard wrote to the first president inquiring about the genealogy of the Washingtons. The president responded in writing, "This is a subject to which I confess to have paid very little attention." Surely, if the stars on the flag were in any way tied to Washington, he would have known about it. Lowes not only was off base on this point, but also in attributing to Washington words in the Declaration of Independence written by Thomas Jefferson.

Lowes's viewpoint, that *everything* American must somehow, in truth, be British, had a flipside of sorts; namely that everything American must be silly. Writing in 1780, Captain Smythe, one of the king's officers, can barely contain his contempt for the new country.

Thirteen is a number peculiarly belonging to the rebels. A party of naval prisoners lately returned from Jersey say that the rations among the rebels are thirteen dried clams a day . . . that Mr. Washington has thirteen toes to his feet (the extra ones having grown since the Declaration of Independence), and the same number of teeth in each jaw . . . that it takes thirteen Congress paper dollars to equal one penny sterling . . . that a well-organized rebel household has thirteen children, all of whom expect to be generals and members of the high and mighty Congress of the "thirteen united States" when they attain thirteen years; that Mrs. Washington has a mottled tomcat (which she calls in a complimentary way Hamilton) with thirteen yellow rings around his tail, and that his flaunting it suggested to the Congress the adoption of the same number of stripes for the rebel flag.

To his credit, George III (who suffered from porphyria and, it is thought, periodic bouts of insanity as a symptom of same) reacted in more dignified manner than his subjects. George III was sitting for portrait artist Benjamin West when he received news of the Declaration of Independence. Years later, West recalled, "He was agitated at first, then sat silent and thoughtful; at length, he said, 'Well, if they cannot be happy under my government, I hope that they may not change it for a worse. I wish them no ill.' "

WHEN YOU TUNE IN TO the World Series in October, one of the television announcers will likely say at the start of the series that the stadium "looks resplendent in the traditional red, white, and blue bunting," referring to the material draped about the ballpark in lieu of the flag. Those bits of decorative cloth are more accurately referred to as *fans,* just like the peanut-eating mob assembled in the ballpark. *Bunting* is the material used to make flags, and this was the case when the first Stars and Stripes surfaced. Today, flags are made chiefly of either cotton or nylon. During revolutionary times, a loose weave of wool bunting was used for the bulk of the flag. The bunting was made in England, the greatest of the seafaring nations, and was imported into the U.S. right up until the Civil War. Even during the Revolution, bunting made its way from England and, eventually, into the hands of flagmakers. The supplies came via the Caribbean islands, likely on board French and Dutch ships.

The bunting was dyed blue with indigo, and red, in all probability, with some concoction of berry juice. The stars were often fashioned from unbleached cotton, which was more tightly woven than the bunting. On flags for use outdoors—which would have been the majority of flags made by Betsy Ross and other seamstresses in Philadelphia—the attaching of the stars was the most time-consuming part of making a flag. (There were several women who advertised their services as flagmakers in the Philadelphia newspapers at the time, so there must have been enough work to go around and enough to afford to advertise.) The stars were cut by hand (indeed, part of the Ross legend is that she demonstrated to her congressional visitors how to create a five-pointed star in a single snip), and probably made *en masse.*

In the workshop, faced with a pile of white stars and a blue piece of bunting, the sewer had two options. The star could be stitched to one side of the blue canton, then the reverse side could be snipped out inside the stitches. This meant that the star on the reverse side would show through slightly smaller. The other option: a canton sandwich between two slices of star. Two separate stars were matched up on either side of the canton and sewn simultaneously. Either way, it was tedious, and attempting to arrange the stars in a perfect circle was time-consuming. The natural result of this was to look for a way to cut down on the time spent creating circles of stars, and the obvious answer was to arrange them in rows. For the duration of the revolution and beyond, flags with rows of stars were in wide use; the two most common formats were rows of four-five-four and three-two-three-two-three.

The vagueness of the congressional wording of the original flag resolution, the time required to fashion circles of stars, and the fact that people sometimes cobbled together a flag with whatever happened to be handy, led to a hodgepodge of flags, including the Continental Colors, flying at various times throughout the war. However, they were all American flags, even if not in the textbook sense. Famous renderings of war scenes—battles and surrenders—frequently show the Stars and Stripes; the stars in such paintings frequently appear as a circle, sometimes in an oval, and, occasionally, as in Trumbull's take on Burgoyne's surrender to Washington at Saratoga, in a square around the edges of the canton. These paintings were always done many years after the fact, however, and are subject to the artist's imaginative powers, even if, as was often the case with Trumbull, the artist was on the scene.

Examples of the wide range of variations on the common theme of the Stars and Stripes are plentiful. A banner carried at the Battle of Brandywine just three months after the flag resolution was passed consisted of a red field and a miniflag in the canton. The flag in the canton has thirteen stripes—seven white and six red—and thirteen multipointed red stars arranged in rows upon its own minicanton. This flag was a military color—not a national flag—but is very possibly the first Stars and Stripes design to fly amidst volleys of musket shot and bayonets. It is one of the few revolutionary era flags extant, and today it is in the collection of the Independence National Historical Park in Philadelphia.

On August 16, 1777, General John Stark's troop of Americans locked horns with the British at Bennington, Vermont. Stark's men carried a green flag with a blue canton and jumbled rows of thirteen five-pointed stars. For many years, it was thought that another more famous flag was on the field that day in Bennington. That flag, which is still made and sold today and among alternatives to the current flag is second in popularity only to the Betsy Ross flag, featured thirteen stripes, seven of them white, including the top and bottom stripes. In the canton, the numeral 76 has an arc of eleven seven-pointed stars over it; there is a single star in each of the upper corners of the canton. Had that flag, known widely as the Bennington Flag, been on the field that day, it would have been the earliest known version of the Stars and Stripes to see battle. In later years, however, textile experts examined the flag and determined it was made in the nineteenth century. "It makes sense when you think about it," says Smith. "Why, in 1777, would you put 76 on a flag. It was just a year and didn't mean anything like it does today. It's only in later years that 1776 becomes significant to us as a year." The Bennington flag never was and, so, still isn't, an official American flag.

The popular Bennington Flag was thought to have been the earliest version of the Stars and Stripes to see battle, but was later determined to have been created in the nineteenth century.

• • •

FOR SHEER FLAG DRAMA, it's difficult to top September 23, 1779—the day John Paul Jones and the *Bonhomme Richard*, flying the Stars and Stripes, traded cannonballs at close range with the British *Serapis* for hours within sight of the British coast. The *Richard* was taking a beating and began to sink when the captain of the *Serapis* called upon Jones to surrender. "I have not yet begun to fight," retorted Jones.

Jones maneuvered his ship even closer to the enemy, and lashed the bowsprit (the long pointy thing at the front of a ship) of the *Serapis* to the *Richard*'s mizzenmast (the mast aft of the main mast). As the battle raged, the Stars and Stripes was shot away and drifted into the sea. Without hesitation, James Bayard Stafford, one of Jones's volunteers, leaped into the ocean and retrieved the flag. Back on the *Richard*, Stafford attempted to raise the flag and was slashed by the sword of a British officer. The Americans won the battle when one of Jones's sailors tossed a grenade into a gunpowder magazine on the *Serapis*. Jones took over the *Serapis* and raised the Stars and Stripes over her. It was a landmark moment for the flag, and was memorialized in the following lines from a poet named Freneau:

> *Go on, great man, to scourge the foe,*
> *And bid the haughty Britons know*
> *They to our thirteen stars shall bend;*
> *The stars that, clad in dark attire,*
> *Long glimmered with the feeble fire,*
> *But radiant now ascend.*

Preble cites a curious footnote to the story, however. The flag survived; so, too, did Stafford. Jones gave Stafford the flag, and his widow passed it to their daughter, Sarah. The flag was photographed for posterity in 1872, and a sketch of it in Preble's book reveals that the haughty Britons did not bend to thirteen stars; there were only twelve stars on the flag, arranged in four rows of three, devastating the meter of Freneau's poem. Whoever made the flag didn't leave enough room in the canton for the final star. During the Civil War, a swatch of this flag was given to Abraham Lincoln at the request of the Stafford family. It was just one of many American flags that figured in the life and death of Lincoln. (According to Smith, the flag's history is spurious; however, it fooled a lot of people—including Preble—for a long time.)

By 1792, with the addition of Vermont and Kentucky, there were fifteen United States. There was considerable debate over the possibility of revising the American flag to reflect the addition of the new states. The senate suggested a change to fifteen stars and fifteen stripes, but the members of the House of Representatives weren't impressed. On January 7, 1794, the record shows that "Mr. Goodhue thought it a trifling business, which ought not to engross the attention of the House, when it was its duty to discuss matters of infinitely greater consequence. If we alter the flag from thirteen to fifteen stripes, and two additional stars . . . we may go on adding and altering at this rate for one hundred years to come. It is very likely that before fifteen years elapse we shall consist of twenty states. The flag ought to be permanent."

Others concurred: "Mr. Thatcher ridiculed the idea of being at so much trouble on a consummate piece of frivolity

. . . he was sorry to see the House take up its time with such trifles."

"Mr. Smith said that this alteration would cost him five hundred dollars, and every vessel in the Union sixty dollars. He could not conceive what the senate meant by sending them such bills. He supposed it was for want of something better to do . . . let the flag be permanent."

(These comments leave little doubt regarding the likelihood that a congressional committee ever paid a visit to Betsy Ross. They also beg the question: Where have all the thrifty congressmen gone?)

Despite the spirited objections of many, the idea was eventually pushed through by those who did not wish to offend the citizens of the two new states. On January 13, 1794, the bill was passed: "Be it enacted, &c, That from and after the first day of May, one thousand seven hundred and ninety-five, the flag of the United States be fifteen stripes, alternate red and white; that the union be fifteen stars, white in a blue field."

Once again, the lack of specificity in the language led to some creative interpretation. One surviving flag from the era, now owned by the Museum of Our National Heritage in Lexington, Massachusetts, has an oval of stars in the canton, and white stripes at the top and bottom of the field. The Revenue Cutter Service introduced the national flag it was going to use in 1799; its stripes were vertical.

The typical design, however, featured five rows of three stars each. One flag made in this pattern was the giant, 32 foot × 40 foot, garrison flag that was raised over Baltimore's Fort McHenry on September 14, 1814—the Star-Spangled Banner.

3

O SAY THAT EASY, efficient, and affordable tools of communication are ubiquitous in the modern world is akin to saying there's a lot of water in the oceans. Communication is accomplished with such electronic ease today that it's impossible for almost anyone to accurately comprehend how difficult it was to quickly communicate *anything* beyond shouting distance in bygone times; before telephones, before telegraphs and radio and mile upon mile of wire, there were handwritten and hand-delivered messages. And there were flags.

The combination of height, color, and movement made flags practical and effective tools for communicating. Navies devised flag-signaling vocabularies and, if an unusual word was necessary, it could be spelled out. In 1805, the one-eyed, one-armed Lord Admiral Nelson used flags to send the most famous message in naval history as the action at Trafalgar commenced: "England expects every man will do his duty." Nelson originally wanted to use the word "confides" rather than "expects," but his flag lieutenant pointed out to him that "confides" would have to be spelled out letter by letter, whereas "expects" was part of the signaling vocabulary. As it was, the word "duty" had to be spelled out frantically just before the subsequent flag signal ordering the fleet to close action. Every man did do his duty, including Nelson, who was mortally wounded.

The hoisting of a flag ensured that it could be seen and also created a physical sense of awe when the observer craned his neck to view it. Movement was the most powerful of the flag's communicative characteristics; the stretching out of a flag in the wind made it easier to see, and the floating motion often created an emotional mirage that made the flag seem like a living thing. This sense of a living flag was realized as early as the year 200 by the use of dragon flags on the field of battle, which were common through the fifteenth century. These flags, essentially windsocks shaped like dragons, with a metal head attached, came alive as they were marched into battle, rocking back and forth in the wind. A reed was attached to it so the wind would make a screeching sound that seemed to emanate from the dragon. From a distance, when the opposing force could not see the pole holding the dragon up, the approaching horde appeared to have supernatural powers. Suddenly, the idea of clashing with a group of weapon-wielding psychos accompanied by a flying dragon didn't seem wise.

The presence and importance of flags at sea and on coastal fortifications, and the perception of a flag as a living entity, are backstory for the garrison flag at Fort McHenry, near the port of Baltimore, Maryland, on September 13 and 14, 1814.

When war broke out with Great Britain in 1812, President James Madison decided the way to get the public involved was to "throw forward the flag of the country, sure that people would press on and defend it." Had the president meant to literally "throw forward the flag" he could have turned to one of his footmen and ordered them to fetch a flag from the Navy or a closet in the White House; the populace at large, however, did not have flags waiting in the closet to be displayed. The Stars and Stripes hadn't been widely used during the Revolutionary War (in fact, it's even difficult for vexillologists to say for certain whether it was used on the battlefield at all) and, while it was acceptable for private citizens to display the American flag, it was not a common sight. Ships and forts were the primary venues for use of the fifteen-star and fifteen-stripe flag in 1812. In short, there were not a lot of American flags to "throw forward."

At Fort McKinley, the garrison possessed an enormous version of the Stars and Stripes measuring 32 feet deep and nearly 43 feet wide. (For the sake of comparison, the huge American flags often seen today flying over car dealerships and other businesses trying to attract attention are one of two sizes: 20 feet × 30 feet or 30 feet × 60 feet.) Colonel George Armistead, the commandant of Fort McHenry, asked the general in charge of defending Baltimore, Sam Smith, to provide a flag. Mary Pickersgill, a descendant of one of the early flagmakers from Philadelphia, was hired to do the work. Along with her daughter, Caroline, Pickersgill got busy. The size of the flag required commensurate work space, so Pickersgill received permission from a local brewer to use the floor of the malt house to spread out her creation. Pickersgill arranged the stars in five staggered rows of three.

Francis Scott Key, a lawyer, was aboard one of His Majesty's ships to negotiate the release of a friend taken prisoner by the British. From shipboard Key looked on as Fort McHenry was bombarded throughout the night of September 13, 1814. Legend has it that the flag Pickersgill made waved over the fort throughout the shelling, and was even pierced by bits of flying debris and shrapnel. The flag could withstand such punishment because Pickersgill and her daughter had made sure the heading of the flag (the part that attaches to the halyard) was extra strong. An account by a British sailor after the fight, however, indicated that a smaller flag stood over the fort for the duration of the battle, and only when the British withdrew was the Pickersgill flag raised. Either way, it was the larger flag that Francis Scott Key saw on the morning of September 14, its size making it visible from a distance.

Key, who, in addition to practicing law, was something of a poet, was moved by the sight of the flag still flying defiantly after facing the best the British Navy had to offer. To capture the moment, Key scribbled down some notes and, later that day, in a hotel room in Baltimore, wrote a poem called "The Defense of Fort McHenry." His friend, Judge Joseph J. Nicholson, was the one who suggested that setting the poem to music might inspire a surge of patriotism. For accompaniment to Key's words, Nicholson suggested "Anacreon in Heaven." Anacreon was an ancient Greek poet; the Anacreontic Society of London used "Anacreon in Heaven," written by John Stafford Smith, as its theme song. It was a well-known and popular ditty, light hearted and, truth be known, a drinking song. The poem appeared in the *Baltimore Patriot*

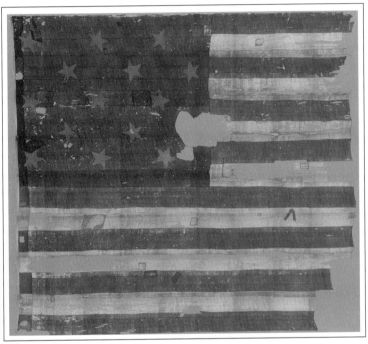

Inspired by what he dubbed the "Star-Spangled Banner," the enormous flag flying over Baltimore's Fort McHenry that withstood repeated volleys of British shelling, Francis Scott Key wrote the words to what would eventually become our national anthem.

newspaper a week later, on September 20. The next day, Thomas Carr, the organ player at St. Paul's Espiscopal Church in Baltimore, hammered out the first live performance of the song. People liked it, especially Key's description of the American flag as "that star-spangled banner." The song grew in popularity over the years, but it was not until more than one hundred years later, in 1931, that "The Star-Spangled Banner" officially became the national anthem of the United States. The flag made by Pickersgill and immortalized by Key thus became *the* Star-Spangled Banner, and although Key used those words to describe the flag in the generic sense, there is only one upper-case Star-Spangled Banner. It is with us still, and is the most popular attraction at the Smithsonian in Washington, D.C., where, as of this writing, it is undergoing restoration at a cost of millions of dollars.

The deep emotional attachment that generations of future Americans would feel for the flag was helped along by the fact that "The Defense of Fort McHenry" was set to music. Poems were a dime a dozen in those days, but they didn't make any more of a connection with the masses than they do today. Music appeals to people on a much wider level; "The Defense of Fort McHenry" would have vanished into poetic oblivion had it not been for the tune. As it was, the song suggested words to describe emotions that Americans could point to as commonly held beliefs about their country: It was the land of the free and the home of the brave; its people were tough and resilient, and would fight to defend their freedom. As the song grew in popularity, and the words to its first stanza became familiar to all, it became more and more clear that the Stars and Stripes could be something beyond just a symbol. They also told the story of the character—the fundamental makeup—of the still very new American people.

AS AMERICA LEARNED during the Vietnam conflict, war doesn't always draw the country closer together. The War of 1812 came as a spinoff of Britain's wars with Napoleonic France: Napoleon, and the British in response, sought to curb free trade on the high seas, and this had a negative impact on the blossoming American economy. That the British had been forcing captured American sailors to serve in the Royal Navy for several years prior to 1812 added to the combustible situation; Madison was urged toward war by impassioned young congressmen who came to be known as the *war hawks*. The New England states vehemently opposed the war, despite the fact that they represented the center of the nation's shipping economy and stood to lose the most financially. There was even a plan put forth that threatened the secession of those states, a threat serious enough to be a major factor in ending the war in 1814. The New Englanders felt the government had bullied the country into war and, early in the conflict, the popular and derogatory image of the federal government as Uncle Sam evolved. The persona of Uncle Sam, it is thought, evolved from the initials U.S. stamped on government property. In time, when Uncle Sam took form as an image, he was cloaked in the Stars and Stripes. The first known image of Uncle Sam appeared in 1832. He was not the tall, bearded, older fellow who later became so familiar.

Rather, he was young, clean shaven, and wrapped in an American flag while seated in a chair. Next to him was Andrew Jackson, who was entangled in an attempt to close down the Bank of the United States, and had just opened a vein in an effort to bleed him dry.

Not quite sixty years old at the time of the Uncle Sam and Andrew Jackson lithograph, the Stars and Stripes had taken the first steps toward being appropriated for motives beyond patriotism. Every American knew what the flag looked like, and its meaning was (for the time at least) straightforward. The image of the flag was too obvious a tool for manipulating public thought for it to escape use by those who sought to sway the opinion of the citizenry; as a group, the largest personal gain stood to be made by politicians, whose use of the flag eventually diluted and complicated its meaning in the minds of the people.

Given the future use of the flag by politicians for reasons devoid of altruism, it is mildly amusing to recall that many members of Congress thought it folly and a waste of valuable time to argue about updating the flag in 1795 to include two new states. It is equally interesting to review a central point of those who opposed changing the flag at that point, namely that it would lead to an endless cycle of new flags. Those members who pointed out that the new nation could conceivably grow quite quickly were correct: the Star-Spangled Banner over Fort McHenry was emblematic of a fifteen-state union, but when the British torched the White House just prior to sailing up the coast to invest Baltimore, the president who fled the destruction of his residence, Madison, was the chief executive of *eighteen* United States, including Tennessee, Ohio, and Louisiana. By the end of 1817, there were two more states: Indiana and Mississippi.

When the subject of once again changing the flag to incorporate the now-larger country was raised in Congress, there was, predictably, disagreement. Peter Wendover, a representative from New York, was the driving force behind updating the Stars and Stripes. Wendover asked Capt. Samuel Reid, who was then living in Washington, to consider a new design for the flag. Reid suggested to Wendover's committee that the number of stripes be reduced to thirteen and that the number of stars be increased to include one for each state. Further, Reid suggested there be three separate flags: one with the stars in rows, for use by the Navy; a special (and odd-looking) flag divided into quarters with the stars in the upper left and the stripes in the lower right, the remaining two quarters having a white background and (upper right) the arms of the United States and (lower left) an image of the Goddess of Liberty. This special flag would fly over Congress and any place the president went. The third flag was for use by private citizens, and on it the stars were formed to create one giant star. Reid's general idea of reducing the stripes to represent the original thirteen states while adding stars to indicate the total number of states seemed plausible. (The idea of the special quartered flag never caught on, but the notion of one giant star did to some degree, especially in later years.)

When the quibbling commenced in earnest over the new flag, it was exasperating. One representative moved to dismiss the idea entirely; another suggested using only seven stars, the idea being that the stripes would represent the original states and the stars the new states; some thought a return

This 1837 banner is an example of the flag design proposed by Samuel Reid for use by ordinary citizens, with the stars in the canton forming one giant star.

to the original thirteen stars and stripes was in order; one member, for reasons unknown, suggested using an arbitrary number of stripes, such as nine or eleven.

Finally, on April 4, 1818, the following act was passed:

> *Sect. 1.* Be it enacted, &c. That from and after the fourth day of July next, the flag of the United States be thirteen horizontal stripes, alternate red and white; that the union have twenty stars, white in a blue field.
>
> *Sect. 2.* And be it further enacted, That on the admission of every new State into the Union, one star be added to the union of the flag; and that such addition shall take effect on the fourth of July next succeeding such admission.

At long last, there was a plan in place to accommodate the inevitable growth of the country into the design of the flag. There were still no specific guidelines regarding the arrangement of the elements that comprised the flag, leaving it open to creative interpretation. The first hint of official specifications for the arrangement of the components of the American flag came from President James Monroe, in 1818. The Navy commissioners at the time created a flag with the stars in four rows of five, but the rows were staggered so that the first star in the second row was in the middle of the first two stars in the first row. Monroe put the kibosh on this idea, ordering that the four rows of stars be stacked evenly one upon the other. For the first time, the Navy, and in later years, the Army, had orders regarding the American flag. The pub-

Before the flag's design was codified, people would arrange the stars in the canton any which way, and the dimensions of the flag varied enormously from banner to banner.

lic was not affected by Monroe's decision; they could and did display American flags with the stars scattered about the canton willy-nilly, often just sewing new stars onto old flags wherever seemed like a good spot for one.

THE SUGGESTION has been made over the years that certain flags hold hypnotic power over anyone who fixes their gaze upon them for more than a few seconds. The flag most commonly associated with such an effect was the swastika-centric flag of Nazi Germany (even though swastikas were used as symbols for millennia before the Nazis latched onto them). The stripes on the American flag can easily render one spellbound, particularly when stretched out on the wind. This effect was used with considerable success in the opening scene of the movie *Saving Private Ryan,* in which the Stars and Stripes are shown fluttering softly over the cemetery in Normandy.

That a flag might possess something along the lines of mystical powers does, of course, depend on who's looking at it. Even if it weren't hypnotic, the Stars and Stripes had a curious effect on people around the world as it started to appear in foreign countries. From 1825 to 1829, Joel Poinsett, from South Carolina, was the U.S. Minister to Mexico. In that time, a disputed election took place, which saw Gomez Pedraza assume the presidency of Mexico. The people revolted, and the action was hottest at a point just a few hundred yards from the home Poinsett occupied. His neighbor, Madame Yturrigaray, was the widow of the viceroy of Mexico. Yturrigaray burst into the Poinsetts' home and beseeched him to protect her house. Just as he was reassuring her, someone out on the street took a shot at him as he stood by the window leading onto a balcony. (It was crazy enough for one man to promise to protect a widow's home against a mob bent on violence. That he stood by the window while doing so makes Mr. Poinsett seem certifiable or, at the very least, an early version of Inspector Clouseau.) The bullet missed, but soon the crowd was storming the residence, clattering at the gates and calling for a cannon (they had overrun an artillery battery) to force entry. The gang had it in for Poinsett because he had frequently offered shelter to European Spaniards—the bad guys—and now he was doing it again. It appeared to be a good time to look for a back door. At this juncture, Poinsett showed why he was the boss by sending the secretary of the American legation, Mr. Mason, onto the balcony with the Stars and Stripes. When Mason wasn't shot, Poinsett joined him on the balcony. In *Origin and History of the American Flag,* George Henry Preble picks up the story from there:

> . . . they both stood on the balcony beneath [the flag's] waving folds. The shouts were hushed, and the soldiers slowly dropped the muzzles of their guns, which were leveled at the balcony and windows. Mr. Poinsett seized this opportunity to tell them who he was, and what flag waved over him, and to claim protection for those who sought security under it. Perceiving the crowd was awed . . . he retired to write and dispatch a note to the commander of the besieging force. The servant entrusted with the note returned and reported the crowd was so great that the

porter was afraid to open the gate for fear the mob of insurgents would rush in. Mr. Poinsett then resolved to go himself, and was joined by Mr. Mason . . . as they stepped over the threshold the crowd rolled back like a wave on the ocean . . .

Eventually, the cavalry saved the day, although it wasn't the U.S. Cavalry.

A SIMILAR SCENE to that in Mexico took place in Portugal in 1836. The home of the American *chargé d'affaires,* a fellow named Brent, was caught in a crossfire during civil strife. Mr. Brent wasn't home at the time, so his wife took charge. Fearing for her family, she took the Stars and Stripes and waved them from the window. The firing stopped.

If the American flag wielded such power over foreigners, its odd magic could certainly be exploited at home. Unluckily for America, the right man for the job was on the scene. He was William Henry Harrison, the ninth president of the United States and not among the sharper knives in the drawer of presidential history. Harrison wasn't in office long enough to learn the name of the White House cook, but he did leave something behind for every American who came after him.

When Harrison ran for the highest office in 1840, his political pedigree was perceived as a liability by those closest to him. He had served four years in the House and four years in the Senate, but his popularity centered around his reputation as an Indian fighter; as governor of the Indiana Territory from 1801 to 1812, Harrison directed forces against a minor attack by Indians at Tippecanoe Creek. This allowed Harrison and his running mate, John Tyler, to use the catchiest election slogan of all time ("Tippecanoe and Tyler Too!"). Harrison's opponent in the race was President Martin Van Buren, and the scheme hatched to wrestle the presidency away from Van Buren would make a modern-day political spinmeister titter: the Harrison campaign would paint Van Buren as an intellectual fop—the sissy boy of the Oval Office. At the same time, Harrison's supporters would point to his tough-guy image: born in a log cabin, their man was not averse to taking a stiff drink with one hand while killing Indians with the other. To drive home their point, Harrison's supporters would do something no politician had done before: make extensive use of the American flag.

It's important to put the election of 1840 into perspective. Unlike today, candidates did not routinely address crowds, for to do so was considered unseemly; the voting men of the era would have considered the candidate a blowhard. Any speaking was done on behalf of the candidate by a second party. There was active campaigning, however, and in Harrison's case this meant displaying lots and lots of American flags. As his supporters dragged model log cabins through the streets and handed out hard cider to thirsty voters, the Stars and Stripes were part of the show. The basic message was that Harrison was a regular guy, but the use of the flag was tinged with an air of the sinister; to use it was to say not only that Harrison was a "real" American, but also to imply that his opponent was something less than that. Thus began an obnoxious trend that is still going strong today.

Harrison won the election, but his inauguration took

place on a nasty day, and tough guy Tippecanoe refused to wear a topcoat. As a result, he caught his death out there. Harrison checked out one month after taking office and was succeeded by Tyler Too!, the first vice president to assume the presidency upon his boss's death.

LIKE IT OR NOT, the history of the American flag is inextricably linked to the nation's wars. The flag was born of the War for Independence and crept into the emotional wellspring of the citizenry, thanks to Mary Pickersgill, Francis Scott Key, and the War of 1812. It is the flag of a united people, and the people are never more united than when the nation is in some way threatened. In their 1999 book, *Blood Sacrifice and the Nation: Totem Rituals and the American Flag,* Carolyn Marvin and David W. Ingle argue that the American flag "is the god of nationalism, and its mission is to organize death." *Blood Sacrifice* is not a beach read; it's a masterfully researched and difficult-to-embrace book that goes to great lengths to prove that the American flag is the totem around which the nation's civic religion revolves, and that "the flag not only symbolizes sacrifice; it demands and receives it as well." The authors of *Blood Sacrifice* explain how they think the flag wields its influence over soldiers in the face of death.

In time of totem danger, the armed forces may also oblige all citizens. The military is the prototype totem group, a model for integrating citizens from all backgrounds into a body with uniform experiences and duties. The commander-in-chief and his agents, including soldiers, comprise the totem class. At the president's word, young men kill and die. Death magic may be directed outward toward the enemy or inward toward totem class members ritually prepared for sacrifice, whichever produces carnage enough for the totem to feast on. . . .

Totem class members model and train for death. In units training for war, commanding officers may direct a certain number of men to step out formation across an imaginary border to signify how many will die before hostilities cease to rehearse totem acolytes in the sacrifice that is expected of them. Sacrificial lambs know their fate. "You put your life on the line to save your country. That's what war's about," explained an Iwo Jima survivor.

It is unlikely that the great majority of America's citizen warriors have viewed their national flag in the same harsh light as Marvin and Ingle (though it should be noted that Ingle served in the U.S. Army *and* Navy). There were no regulations that ordered the carrying of the Stars and Stripes by U.S. land forces in battle until the Mexican War of 1846 to 1848. The Stars and Stripes had been on battlefields before, but never as part of a mandate. Flags had been a part of the battlefield for thousands of years by that point, and the relationship between warriors and flags had evolved into a highly personal one. "The earliest flags on the battlefield tended to be signaling flags," says Whitney Smith. "But, very quickly, when you get a group of men together in a situation that involves life or death, or being maimed or captured, flags take on a significance beyond [signaling]. There were religious characteristics associated with the legitimacy of the state. As a rule, people believed the state was founded on something greater than the power of the ruler or the dynasty, and that power was universally attributed to the gods—the gods wish it. So the flags themselves were blessed by priests, and in the Middle Ages they were mounted on enormous wooden carriages that required two oxen to drag onto the field. A group of guards would stand around the carriage protecting the flag. There is imagery of this type of color guard as far back as Alexander the Great.

"When the fighting was going on, the soldiers would look to the flag: Is it still there? Has it been captured? Is it being dragged away? Aside from having their own skins to save, the soldiers wanted to feel as if the gods were with them, that they were not fighting in vain. A flag like the dragon flag was meant to intimidate, but basically flags served the signaling function and represented the spirit under which a whole enterprise was being undertaken. There were always the elite who led the charge as part of their duty to god and king, but you also had the guys who cooked the meals and dragged the cannons and stood in the last ranks with a pole, hoping they didn't have to hurt somebody with it.

"When professional armies appeared in the Middle Ages, the soldiers were no longer conscripts. Then, for the first time, you start having flags not necessarily associated with a country or a religion and not just for signaling; rather they are associated with individual units. These regimental colors became the repository of a unit's history—a motto, a battle cry or whatnot. So, protecting that regimental flag meant everything. As a soldier, they always faced the idea of dying, and the percentages of dying were horrendous in past wars. They had to feel like they were dying for something. So seeing that standard advance, seeing the national colors advance, was the core of that. Also, there was the question of the alternative: You could always retreat, but unless your commander ordered it, you were a coward—you were going back on the principles you were fighting for. It was the fundamental commitment a soldier had. That's why when Napoleon was defeated by the first coalition in 1814, his soldiers burnt the flag and drank the ashes in wine so they could say, 'These colors never fell to the enemy.'

"The reason young boys were often picked to carry the flag into battle was to inspire the older guys; if a kid can walk into the face of the enemy with no weapon, I can certainly go forward and do my part. There was a guard around those color bearers, and when they were hit, there was no lack of people who grabbed for the flag. It was just a matter of who was nearest; if you saw the color bearer falter, it was simply a matter of honor to be the next to die. You just grabbed it. It gave meaning to death, particularly when you could see the guy you were going to kill if he didn't kill you first."

When the Stars and Stripes marched into Mexico with the U.S. Army in 1846, the soldiers looked upon it in the manner Smith describes. At Chapultepec, Mexico City, American soldiers attacked up a steep incline they called Grasshopper Hill. The Stars and Stripes led the way, carried by Lt. James Longstreet. When Longstreet was wounded, he handed the flag to Lt. George Pickett. Nearly twenty years later, Longstreet and Pickett, who both risked their lives for the Stars and Stripes on Grasshopper Hill, would rank among the most famous Confederate commanders in the Civil War, a conflict that, distilled to its essence, was a fight for the flag.

"What happened was that people looked to the flag unconsciously as the definition of American life," says Smith. "We didn't have a king or an aristocracy, nor a common ethnic background or even a common religion. All of a sudden the Civil War comes along and the whole fate of the nation is up for grabs. And the defense of Fort Sumter raised the question: Would we just say, 'Goodbye and good luck to you. You can have the fort and other federal property you've seized, too.' Or would we say, 'Hell, no, this is a perpetual union, and part of the idea behind it is that we'll work together and solve any problems.' Sumter was the powder keg because lots of forts had been surrendered, but Anderson—the commander there—was not about to surrender the fort. And Lincoln backed him up. So, even though the relief ships were turned back and the families of the soldiers were removed, the decision was made to defend the fort, a piece of U.S. property. So, it was a defense of the flag and the war became a fight for the flag, and it was expressed in those terms. The flag was everywhere. Every school flew a flag and prior to that there is only one known instance—in 1817—of a school flying an American flag. Union soldiers even carried miniature flags called Bible flags, small enough to fit into the Bible they would take with them to the battlefield. The start of the Civil War was the beginning of the sense we have today of the American flag as an everyday object and of something that belongs to everyone."

4

Every city, town and village suddenly blossomed with banners. On forts and ships, from church spires and flag staffs, from colleges, hotels, store fronts and private balconies, from public edifices, everywhere the old flag was flung out, and everywhere it was hailed with enthusiasm; for its prose became poetry, and there was seen in it a sacred value which it had never before possessed . . . Every window-shutter is tied with the inevitable red, white and blue, and dogs, even, are wrapped in the star-spangled banner . . .

The demand for flags was so great that the manufacturers could not furnish them fast enough. Bunting was exhausted, and recourse was had to all sorts of substitutes. In New York, the demand for flags raised the price of bunting from $4.75 a piece to $28, and book-muslin, used for the stars and usually worth six to ten cents, was sold for $3 a yard. Loyal women wore miniature banners in their bonnets, and blended the colors with almost every article of dress; and men carried the emblem on breast-pins and countless other devices. The patchwork of red, white and *blue, which had flaunted in their faces for generations without exciting much emotion, in a single day stirred the pulses of the people to battle, and became the inspiration of national effort. All at once the dear old flag meant the Declaration of Independence; it meant Lexington; it meant Bunker Hill and Saratoga . . . it meant freedom; it meant the honor and life of the republic . . .*

The flag of the republic—how dear to those who were true to it they never knew till then—was raised . . . by spontaneous impulse, upon every staff which stood on loyal ground; from the [Great] Lakes to the Potomac, from the shores of the Atlantic to the banks of the Mississippi, the eye could hardly turn without meeting the bright banner which symbolized . . . in its stars the growth and glory of the nation and government which insurgents had banded together to destroy.

—GEORGE HENRY PREBLE, on the reaction to the bombardment and evacuation of Fort Sumter in 1861, from *Origin and History of the American Flag*

HEN SOUTHERN GUNS OPENED up on Fort Sumter, in Charleston, South Carolina, on April 12, 1861, the attack was not a surprise. That date and event are acknowledged as the official start to the Civil War, but the country had been drifting toward war for years; during the early months of 1861 the only question that remained was when the war would begin. South Carolina seceded from the United States on December 10, 1860 and in the first three weeks of January 1861, Florida, Mississippi, and Georgia followed. The whole country knew Fort Sumter was a point of contention; for months leading up to the cannonade on April 12, newspapers carried stories about the fort. On February 2, the *New York Times* ran the headlines:

A Lieutenant in the Navy Treated by the Floridians as a Prisoner of War

Expectation of an Attack on Fort Sumter

Immense Preparations at Charleston

Major Robert Anderson, commander of the Federal garrison at Sumter, knew full well what was in store for him. On Christmas Eve, 1860, he wrote to a friend in Boston, who, in turn, gave the letter to the *Boston Journal:*

> *When I inform you that my garrison consists of only sixty effective men, that we are in a very indifferent work, the walls of which are only about fourteen feet high, and that we have, within 100 yards of our wall, sand hills which command our work, and which afford admirable sites for our batteries, and the finest covers for sharp-shooters, and that, besides this, there are numerous houses, some of them within pistle-shot, you will at once see that if attacked in force, headed by any one but a simpleton, there is scarce a possibility of our being able to hold out long enough to enable our friends to come to our succor.*

Trusting that God will not desert us in our hour of trial, I am, very sincerely yours.

Robert Anderson, Major First Artillery

Many of the letters Anderson wrote leading up to April ended up in newspapers (something he made clear he wasn't happy about), and fueled widespread sympathy for his plight. Meanwhile, that the Stars and Stripes would define the coming war was, like the inevitability of an attack on Fort Sumter, apparent before April. John A. Dix was the brand new head of the U.S. Treasury Department in January 1861 and he was concerned about secessionists seizing control of ships under his authority. Dix sent one of his underlings, William Hemphill Jones, to Mobile, Alabama, and New Orleans to see that two such ships, the *Lewis Cass* and the *Robert McClelland*, did not fall into enemy hands. By the time Jones reached Mobile, the *Lewis Cass* had already been surrendered. Jones went to New Orleans and informed Captain Breshwood of the *McClelland* that he was not to surrender the ship, but Breshwood refused to take orders from the Treasury Department. Jones telegraphed Dix in Washington for further direction. Dix fired off the following wire, which he wrote in his own hand:

Treasury Department

Jan. 29, 1861

Tell Lieut. Caldwell to arrest Capt. Breshwood, assume command of the Cutter and obey the order I gave through you. If Capt. Breshwood after arrest undertakes to interfere with the command of the Cutter, tell Lieut. Caldwell to consider him a mutineer & treat him accordingly. If any one attempts to haul down the American flag, shoot him on the spot.

> *John A. Dix*
> *Secretary of the Treasury*

The cable was intercepted; Jones never received it and Breshwood raised the flag of Louisiana in place of the American flag. Dix later said he wrote the note in "haste and with a bad pen," but he was not the only one whose emotions regarding the flag were running hot.

All over the country, the Stars and Stripes were under siege, often being replaced by the Palmetto flag of South Carolina, which had been adopted for use by many secessionists. On February 21, the *New York Times* reported from Nebraska.

Excitement at Nebraska City

Nebraska City, Tuesday, Feb. 19.

Old Fort Kearney was taken possession of last night by a party of Secessionists, and this morning a Palmetto flag waves over the fortress, bearing the inscription "Southern Rights."

Great excitement prevails, and efforts are being made to take the fort by the Union party.

Later—An attack was made on the Fort this morning at 10 o'clock, and amid great excitement, the Palmetto

Courtesy of the Museum of the Confederacy, Richmond, Virginia

The flag of the Fifth South Carolina Infantry (featuring the palmetto tree of the state flag) symbolized the defiance found throughout the South during the Civil War.

flag was torn down and the Stars and Stripes raised in its place.

Fort Kearney, Wednesday, Feb. 20.

The telegraphic report that at old Fort Kearney the Palmetto flag was raised, does not apply to the present new Fort Kearney, where Col. Miles commands, and, if I understand his views, and the temper of his troops, before the Stars and Stripes are ever hauled down, every man will die at the foot of the flag-staff.

Letter writers to the *Times* were furious over the wave of assaults against the Stars and Stripes. Wrote one man who identified himself only as a Douglas Democrat:

Palmetto flag! *When my father told his children the story of the Revolution, (in which for eight years he bore arms), and when he endeavored to bequeath his patriotism, did we ever hear him talk of a Connecticut flag, a New York flag or a New Jersey flag? What but a national emblem ever inspired their hopes of the greatness and glory of the country.*

It is the Nation, not the States, that has been and is still the hope of the world . . .

A writer from California was more blunt:

California is upright, downright and outright for the Union, whatever its legislature may say or do. No buzzard, bat, owl, pelican, nigger, bear, [or] wolf flag shall ever flap treason from its folds, while there lives a pioneer to pull it down.

Yours in the bonds of Union,
John H. Turney

The man standing squarely in the center of the national maelstrom was President-elect Abraham Lincoln. Between his election and inauguration, Kansas had been admitted to the union as the thirty-fourth state (January 29, 1861). Even though the flag wasn't officially changed to reflect the new state until July 4, 1861, there was a 34-star flag on hand for Lincoln himself to raise on Washington's Birthday (February 22) when he stopped in Philadelphia on the way to Washington.

Under the headline "He Raises an American Flag with Thirty-Four Stars," the *New York Times* told the story of the scene that morning in Philadelphia, where Lincoln stood on the same ground as the men who founded the country less than one hundred years before.

The ceremony of raising the flag of thirty-four stars over the Hall of Independence this morning, by Mr. Lincoln, was attended with the solemnity due such an occasion, the scene being an impressive one. At the rising of the sun crowds of people streamed from all parts of the city towards the State House, and very soon every inch of ground was occupied, a vast number of ladies being present.

Lincoln, the all-time heavyweight champion of short oratory, addressed the crowd in an impromptu speech which painted an eerily accurate picture of the coming years.

I am filled with deep emotion at finding myself standing here in this place, where were collected together the wisdom, the patriotism, the devotion to the principle from which sprang the institutions under which we live . . . I have never had a feeling, politically, that did not spring from the sentiment embodied in the Declaration of Independence. I have pondered over the dangers which were incurred by the men who assembled here, and framed and adopted that Declaration of Independence . . . It was not the mere matter of the separation of the Colonies from the mother land, but that sentiment in the Declaration of Independence which gave liberty, not alone to the people of this country, but, I hope, to the world, for all future time. It was that which gave promise that in due time the weight would be lifted from the shoulders of all men . . . Now, my friends, can this country be saved upon that basis? If it can, I will consider myself one of the happiest men in the world—if I can help to save it. If it cannot be saved upon that principle it will be truly awful. But if this country cannot be saved without giving up that principle, I was about to say, I would rather be assassinated on this spot than surrender it . . .

My friends, this is wholly an unexpected speech, and I did not expect to be called upon to say a word when I came here. I supposed it was merely to do something towards raising the flag—I may therefore have said something indiscreet. I have said nothing but what I am willing to live by, and if the pleasure of Almighty God, die by.

Today, convenience has trumped meaning and Washington's birthday has been lumped together with Lincoln's on Presidents' Day, when the two are thought of as nothing more than an excuse for a day off from work and school. In 1861, Washington's birthday was a *big* deal; on February 23, the *New York Times* ran multiple front page stories on the celebration around the country, including those in its own city.

> *Brightly rose the sun yesterday morning, and its first beam gilded the tips of countless mastheads in the harbor and many a flagstaff throughout all the City, the flag of the Union leaped forth upon the westerly breeze and fluttered with joy at the omen. Never we venture to say, were so many American banners hoisted in the Metropolis. Not only on the roofs of the public buildings and hotels, but also on other places of business, without number, and wherever elsewhere there was a pole to fling it forth from our flag was there. And never was the beauty of the Stars and Stripes so fully recognized, and loyalty to the "land of the free," which it floats over, so generally given a public expression . . .*

The first flag boom was underway in America. When Lincoln was inaugurated on March 4, 1861, a weird thing happened to the American flag flying over the Capitol. The *New York Times* writer attending the inauguration noticed it. "Early in the forenoon, when the flag was unfurled upon the Capitol, one of the halliards [sic] gave way, and, splitting in two, the flag flung out like a pennant. For a long while it could not be taken down, though finally an adventurous man climbed to the top of the staff and, tearing away the ill-omened standard, replaced it with an entire flag of the Union." The attack on Sumter was still a month in the future.

The halyards that held the Stars and Stripes aloft over Sumter were severed by enemy fire early in the bombardment. The flag stayed put, but was entangled to the point whereby it could not be raised or lowered. According to Preble's account of the battle, the flag staff was hit by fire eight times before it gave way and the national colors fell "down through the smoke among the gleaming embers." The fort's defenders reacted quickly; the flag was snatched up before it caught fire, and rushed back up to the ramparts. In a storm of flying steel, the flag was nailed to the small bit of remaining staff (the halyards were useless) and fastened to the wall of the fort with the aid of a mason from Baltimore, named Lyon. Later reports averred that the flag had been lowered to half mast by the defenders, but Major Anderson discounted this by saying, "God Almighty nailed that flag to the mast, and I could not have lowered it if I tried."

When the firing ceased, 3,000 rounds had been fired at Sumter, yet not a single soldier had been killed on either side. Anderson agreed to evacuate the fort—not an official surrender—as long as he could take the flag with him. The only ca-

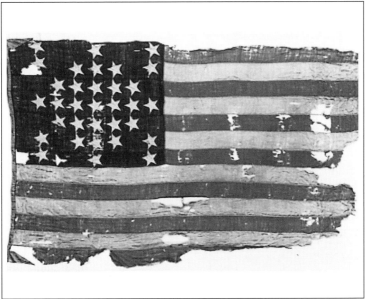

This small "storm" flag flew throughout the firefight at Fort Sumter. When Federal troops departed the fort, they took their flags with them.

sualties of the event occurred as the Union men fired a salute to their flag immediately prior to departure. As the flag was raised again over the ramparts, a pile of ammunition near one of the guns was touched off, killing one man on the spot and mortally wounding another.

In the immediate aftermath, South Carolina's Governor Pickens addressed an assembled crowd in the streets of Charleston. "Thank God the war is open," said Pickens, "and we will conquer or perish. We have humbled the flag of the United States. I can say to you, it is the first time in the history of this country that the stars and stripes have been humbled. That proud flag was never lowered before to any nation on earth. We have lowered it in humility before the Palmetto and Confederate flags; and we have compelled them to raise by their side the white flag, and ask for an honorable surrender. The flag of the United States has triumphed for seventy years; but today, the 13th of April, it has been humbled, and humbled before the glorious little State of South Carolina."

Them was fightin' words.

THE FLAG FEVER that gripped the country was perceived as something of a phenomenon even as it happened. The grip of the flag was inescapable and tremendous in its strength. Once the Civil War was officially underway, any vagueness that had existed about the flag's meaning was swept away in the fervor. On May 6, 1861, an editorial writer for the *New York Times* acknowledged the new omnipresence of the flag, and the mixed emotions it drew forth, in an opinion entitled simply, "The Stars and Stripes."

It is related in Baltimore, that one of the wounded Massachusetts men—a mere youth—after the fight with the mob, crept into a shop and was kindly sheltered by the owner, and on being questioned why so young a man as he came so far with arms, he murmured faintly, but "with a simple affection" the account says, with dying breath, "The Stars and Stripes."

If any one goes around among our soldiers now, and asks many the reason of their enlisting, they will very probably say, "It was the insult to the old Flag at Sumter," or, "it is for the Stars and Stripes." Many unreflecting people laugh at this as an ignorant enthusiasm. But it is not. Who that knows human history or human nature, can doubt in regard to the power of an emblem. For eighteen centuries, the hopes of humanity, its highest life and its pledge of immortality have been in a symbol—the gallows of a past time, the Cross of the modern ages. That simple emblem is a reality—it contains history and a promise in itself.

So with the tri-color: wherever a Frenchman looks upon it, he sees not merely the three bands of color, but a whole history of glory and civilization. So with the red cross—the Englishman reads in it a thousand years of sturdy manhood and indomitable vigor.

So with our glorious Stars and Stripes. Who that has seen it waving in foreign ports, amid the emblems of bigotry and tyranny; or has beheld it gleaming of late on some border-town, where to display it was danger and perhaps death; or who that saw its tattered folds sweep out from the flag-staff at Sumter in the iron hands of Wash-

*ington in our own city, has not sometime felt his eyes fill
with tears, as he gazed at it. It is our great Emblem. It
symbolizes the American Idea. Of late years, indeed, it has
covered so much baseness, and oppression, and treason,
that the love of our people for it was growing cold. But
now, in the time of its peril, when the shot of traitors have
pierced it, when it is discarded and outcast by those who
have so long used it to protect their iniquities, the feeling
of the people springs towards it like a passion. It represents
all that we have loved and hoped for in America. It is the
symbol of Equal Rights, of Law, of Country, and, above
all, Universal Liberty. Thank God! its stains are washed
away. It is now an emblem of the most advanced humanity; of shelter to the oppressed; of free speech; of the inalien-
able rights of man; of well-ordained and lawful freedom.
It is the white plume of Civilization in its direful battle
with Barbarism, on this Western Continent. The hopes
and prayers of mankind follow it. As we look at its gay
flaunting, we see in it a short but noble history; the heroic
war of Independence, the wise building of the Constitution, the growth of a great and prosperous nation, which
should shame all ancient governments, and secure Justice
and Liberty for all men of every creed and condition.*

*The Stars and Stripes are but beginning their glori-
ous career. They shall yet wave over Richmond and
Charleston, and Mobile and New Orleans. They shall go
on over new lands and new seas. They shall be the herald
and the banner of civilization and humanity for many a
coming century. All men shall look to them as the symbol of
liberty.*

> *Therefore, let the glorious banner flaunt from every housetop, from window and chimney, from monument and church—for no place is too sacred for it. In this time of its danger, we will wear it over our breasts, and bear it on our persons; and you who go forth to defend the Flag, remember that nothing can dishonor it but treachery and cowardice! Bear the old Stars and Stripes, as the emblem of our country, before you in battle; count it honor enough that you have been able to bleed and suffer for it, and a sweet and glorious thing if for that Flag you can die.*

Read in an historic vacuum, it is tempting to ascribe those words to someone who today would at the very least be called a jingoist, and, more likely, be considered off his right-wing rocker. Even though we cannot emotionally transport ourselves to May 1861, it is easy enough to understand the passionate hyperbole the flag can cause; it is the nature of perfect love. Perfect love, as anyone who reads romance novels or ponders such weighty issues can tell you, is unconditional—there are no ifs, ands, or buts about it. To love or be loved unconditionally is a very rare state of grace; in times of national peril, expressions of unconditional love of country are more numerous, straightforward and colorful than in ordinary times because a threat to the continuing existence of the country is a threat to the continuing existence of life. In short, it is the only time when the majority of Americans not only set aside their suspicious of government shenanigans but also have renewed (if temporary) and unwavering faith in their leaders; the knee-jerk reaction toward unity between the people, the bodies that govern them and the national symbol that represents them is about survival. This is not an absolute rule—no matter the era or the circumstances, there are always some Americans who think it's preposterous to "rally 'round the flag" (and, to borrow a catch phrase from *Seinfeld*, "not that there's anything wrong with that")—but it does apply to the majority.

Feelings regarding the American flag during the Civil War could not have been anything other than deep seated. The war was *hugely* important to the nation's future; would the country dissolve into a jumble of bickering fiefdoms destined to re-create the endless loop of petty and bloody squabbling that was the legacy of civilization until that time? Or would it thrive in a way *only* possible by the continuance of the union?

The answers to those questions were initially mixed—before Fort Sumter, at least. An editorial in the *New York Tribune* said, "Whenever a considerable section of the Union shall deliberately resolve to go out, we shall resist all coercive measures designed to keep it in. We hope never to live in a republic whereof one section is pinned to the residue by bayonets." And, in a speech in Boston on January 22, 1861, antislavery orator Wendell Phillips declared: "All hail disunion! Sacrifice everything for the Union? God forbid! Sacrifice everything to keep South Carolina in it? Rather, build a bridge of gold and pay her toll over it! Let her march off with banners and trumpets and we will speed the parting guest . . ."

Few people in 1861 were in the mood for such reasoning after Sumter, however; in April, in East Fairhaven, Massachusetts, a man hoisted a flag the rest of the community felt showed sympathy to the secessionist cause. (The flag in question is unknown; possibly it was a Palmetto flag or the brand new national flag of the Confederate States of America, which, according to the *New York Times,* was "pretty generally displayed" in South Carolina by April. That flag, the Stars and Bars, was clearly a derivation of the Stars and Stripes. It had three wide stripes of red, white, red in the field and a blue canton with a circle of eleven white stars, one for each Confederate state. Today the term *Stars and Bars* is often incorrectly used to describe the much more famous Confederate battle flag, but they were two very different banners.) The East Fairhaven man, named Steele, was repeatedly threatened over the flag; he refused to lower it and said he'd shoot anyone who tried to do the same. Eventually, he was physically overpowered and made to walk three miles to the town of Mattapoisett, where his posterior was tarred and feathered. The mob forced him to offer three cheers for the Stars and Stripes, take an oath to support the Constitution, and swear never again to hoist any flag other than the American flag; stories abound of similar incidents throughout the Union at around the same time.

The similarities between the Stars and Stripes and the Stars and Bars were as intentional as those between the Continental Colors and the Union Jack, and for good reason. Despite their desire to break off from the United States, some Southerners justifiably considered the Stars and Stripes to be part of their national identity and heritage, and the Stars and Bars were an historical nod to the American flag. The resemblance of the two flags was too close for the liking of some Southerners, however, and rendered the Stars and Bars practically useless on the battlefield. (The design was modified in

1863, the blue canton replaced with a white one, and the stars replaced with the Confederate battle flag. In 1865, one month before the war ended, a red vertical stripe was added to the fly end of the flag.)

There was never serious consideration on the part of the United States to remove stars from the American flag to reflect the secession of the rebel states. To remove stars would have been an acknowledgment of the legitimacy of the secessionist movement, and there was no intention on the part of Abraham Lincoln or the Congress to make such a concession. By far, the wackiest idea for adjusting the flag to mirror the national feud was put forth by Samuel F. B. Morse, the inventor of the telegraph, and an ardent antiwar activist: "The Southern section is now agitating the question of a device for their distinctive flag," said Morse. "Cannot this question of flags be so settled as to aid in the future union? I think it can. If the country can be divided, why not the flag . . . ? The most obvious solution which springs up in this respect is to divide the old flag, giving half to each. It may be done, and in a manner to have a salutary moral effect upon both parties.

"Let the blue union be diagonally divided, from left to right or right to left, and the thirteen stripes longitudinally, so as to make six and a half stripes in the upper, and six and a half in the lower portion. Referring to it, as on a map—the upper portion being the north, and the lower portion being the south—we have the upper diagonal division of the blue field and the upper six and a half stripes as the Northern Flag, and the lower six and a half stripes for the Southern Flag—the portion of the blue field in each to contain the stars to the number of States embraced in each confederacy.

. . . It prevents all dispute on a claim to the old flag by either confederacy. It is distinctive, for the two cannot be mistaken for each other either at sea, or at a distance on land. [This is true, actually. In the "Northern Flag," the entire lower half of the flag and the lower triangle in the canton would have been all white; the "Southern Flag" would have had less overall white, but the entire upper half, save for the sliver of blue canton and stars, would have been white.] Each being a moiety of the old flag, will retain something, at least, of the sacred memories of the past for the sober reflection of each confederacy. And then, if a war with some foreign nation . . . should unhappily occur . . . under our treaty of offence and defence [sic], the two separate flags, by natural affinity, would clasp fittingly together, and the glorious old Flag of the Union, in its entirety, would again be hoisted, once more embracing all the Sister states . . ."

One can only imagine someone taking Morse aside and whispering to him, "Don't quit your day job, Sam."

AS IN ANY CONFLICT OF ARMS, the Civil War was ultimately decided by the foot soldiers of the two sides. As the Union men marched along the roads and over fields, one of their favorite songs was "The Battle Cry of Freedom," and its famous lines:

Yes, we'll rally 'round the flag, boys
we'll rally once again
shouting the battle cry
of freedom

The highest military award of the United States, the Congressional Medal of Honor, was established during the war to acknowledge bravery on the part of noncommissioned officers and privates. Nearly one thousand of the medals were awarded and, in a great many cases, they were bestowed upon men who had carried the Stars and Stripes into battle or who captured Confederate flags. Carrying a flag into battle or being part of the color guard who protected it was very deadly business; on the first day of fighting at Gettysburg in 1863, a single Michigan Regiment, the 24th, lost nine color bearers. The Sixth Wisconsin Regiment took part in that same battle. One of its officers later recalled the scene as the regiment charged into the rebel lines: "Any correct picture of this charge would represent a V-shaped crowd of men with the colors at the advance point, moving firmly and hurriedly forward. The only commands I gave, as we advanced, were, 'Align on the colors! Close up on that color! Close up on that color!' "

In the equally horrific battle at Antietam, a Union detachment faced the onslaught of the Sixth Georgia regiment. The Union color bearer was George Horton, who had been shot in the arm two days earlier. At Antietam, Horton was hit in the ankle, but refused offers of help from his fellow soldiers, one of whom, an officer, later described the scene. "Horton had gone down. His foot shot off. He had firmly planted the colors in the ground. Several of us begged him to give us the colors, that we might save them."

"Stay and defend them," said Horton.

Horton stood his ground, pistol in hand, as the Georgians rushed him. An enemy soldier fired at Horton from just a few paces away, and killed him.

Tales of the color bearers of the Civil War are as numerous as the regiments themselves. In one case, the color bearer was neither a young boy nor a man: A soldier in the First Rhode Island Regiment was married to a woman named Kady Brownell; and so devoted was Mrs. Brownell to her man and the Union, that she followed the regiment to war. When they made camp, she cooked for the men and washed clothes. At the First Battle of Manassas (Bull Run), legend has it that in the thickest fighting the Stars and Stripes were carried by Kady Brownell.

For the flag to go backwards—to retreat—was out of the question unless ordered. At Vicksburg, 149 men out of a brigade of 150 delayed their charge due to rifle fire and took cover in a deep ravine. The lone man to continue the advance was William Wagden, the color bearer from the Eighth Missouri Regiment. He moved to within twenty yards of the Confederate lines, dug a hole with his bayonet, planted the flag and stayed by it throughout the remainder of the day.

It was left to the Irish-Americans to provide humor in the darkest of times; in a battle in Mississippi, an Indiana regiment was forced to give ground and the Stars and Stripes were left behind as they withdrew to a better position. Upon realizing the banner had been left behind, an Irishman who was part of the color guard sprinted across open ground and singlehandedly assaulted the squad of Confederate soldiers who held the captured flag. Using his rifle butt as a club, he whacked several of the enemy over the head before grabbing the flag and returning to his lines. The man's admiring commander promoted him to sergeant on the field. "Say no more about it, Captain," said the Irishman. "I dropped my whiskey flask among the rebels and went to fetch it back. I thought I might just as well bring the flag along, too."

THE LEGENDARY STORIES of the Stars and Stripes are not confined solely to situations where musket shot and cannonballs were whizzing. In Hagerstown, Maryland, on June 26, 1861, soldiers of the First Wisconsin Regiment assembled for review by their leader, Col. John Starkweather, who challenged them to follow him to their death. Starkweather ordered the regimental colors to be brought forward and placed next to the Stars and Stripes. He knelt before the flags to say a prayer, and one by one, his men, too, knelt at the foot of the flag, pledging to defend it with their lives.

No story, though, stirred the public more than the tale of Barbara Frietchie, the 96-year-old woman in Frederick, Maryland, who allegedly hung the Stars and Stripes from the window of her home as Stonewall Jackson's men occupied the town in September 1862. (The story is questionable, particularly the part about Stonewall Jackson's involvement. But . . .) Confederate soldiers fired a volley at the flag and snapped the staff. Frietchie pulled the flag in, then reappeared in the window holding the stump of the staff and waving the flag, taunting the rebel soldiers. "Fire at this old head, then, boys; it is not more venerable than your flag."

The moment was popularized by John Whittier in the poem *Barbara Frietchie:*

> *Up the street came the rebel tread,*
> *Stonewall Jackson riding ahead.*

Under his slouched hat left and right
He glanced; the old flag met his sight
"Halt!" the dust-brown ranks stood fast
"Fire!" out blazed the rifle blast.
It shivered the window, pane and sash;
It rent the banner with seam and gash.
Quick, as it fell, from the broken staff
Dame Barbara snatched the silken scarf;
She leaned far out on the window-sill,
And shook it forth with royal will
"Shoot if you must this old gray head,
But spare your country's flag," she said.
A shade of sadness, a blush of shame,
Over the face of the leader came;
The nobler nature within him stirred
To life at that woman's deed and word:
"Who touches a hair of yon gray head
Dies like a dog! March on!" he said.

After four years, the Civil War ended with a Union victory. On Monday, April 10, 1865, the *New York Times* carried the following headlines, surrounding an image of the American flag, on the left-hand column of the front page:

HANG OUT YOUR BANNERS
UNION
VICTORY!
PEACE!

Surrender of General Lee and His Whole Army

On page five of the same edition, a brief story appeared under the headline:

Fort Sumter
Departure of the Arago—the Old Flag on Board

At noon on Saturday, the government transport Arago *sailed from the foot of Beech Street, bound for Fort Sumter, the object of her mission being to convey a large party of ladies and gentlemen to witness the restoration of the old flag to the ramparts of the fort.*

By 10 o'clock A.M. those invited commenced to arrive. Gen. Robert Anderson, with his wife, son and three daughters was early on board . . .

So it was that the hero of Sumter, now a general, returned to the place that made him famous, to once again raise the flag that had roused a nation.

Just five days later, the paper reported the assassination of Abraham Lincoln, the man who shouldered the ordeal for the nation. The killer, John Wilkes Booth, was an actor, and after shooting the president in the head, he paused for a big finish. The *Times* reported that Booth appeared in the box where Lincoln was seated at Ford's Theatre "waving a long dagger in his right hand, and exclaiming '*Sic semper tyrannis,*' and immediately leaped from the box, which was in the second tier, to the stage beneath, and ran across to the opposite side, making his escape . . ."

Booth's focus on his big line ("Thus ever to tyrants," the state motto of Virginia) may have diverted his attention from

John Wilkes Booth's leap from the balcony at Ford's Theatre was foiled by the flags bunched up along the front of the presidential box.

his big action scene—the leap to the stage. When Booth pushed off, his foot became entangled in an American flag bunched up for decoration on the front of Lincoln's box. The result of the unplanned free fall was that Booth broke a bone in his leg; the broken leg made fast and prolonged flight impossible, hastening his eventual capture.

Lincoln died in a bed across the street from the theater in the home of a tailor named William Petersen. (Booth had once slept in the same bed when a friend of his was renting the room from Petersen.) The flag's role in the assassination is all the more quirky when this fact is considered: the manner in which the flag was displayed—bunched up—is today considered a violation of the Flag Code.

The most violent years of America's history were over, ended in one last spasm of calamity brought about by a hack actor. On April 17, 1865, a *Times* editorialist closed the chapter for America:

> *When generations have passed away, and the unhappy wounds of this war are healed, and the whole nation is united on a basis of universal liberty, our posterity will read the words of the great Emancipator and leader of people with new sympathy and reverence, thanking God that so honest and so pure a man, so true a friend of the oppressed, and so genuine a patriot, guided the nation in the time of its trial, and prepared the final triumph which he was never allowed to see.*

5

THE WAR TO PRESERVE the United States saw the flag become the primary icon of American life; furthermore, the war made the flag more ubiquitous in America than other national flags were in their own countries, something that remains true to this day. (In a review of *Soldiers: Fighting Men's Lives, 1901–2001,* a book of the recollections of British soldiers by Philip Ziegler, the reviewer James Buchan noted that "in matters of its imperial history Britain struggles with an excruciating inhibition. In Britain, only fascists and skinheads wrap themselves in the Union Jack." More radically, citizens of India were only recently granted the freedom to fly that country's flag.) In what foreigners perceive as typical American self-absorption and Americans themselves see as a celebration of national identity, the Stars and Stripes are front and center in the modern American tableau.

During the Civil War, the flags on battlefields, towns and cities still frequently took on what today appear as aberrant forms: occasionally the stars were formed into the giant star suggested by Reid, for example; blue cantons containing a circle of stars within a larger circle of stars were also in the mix. Flags with the stars fixed in rows became more and more common as the nineteenth century crept along, but it wasn't until 1912 that President William Howard Taft signed an executive order that put in place exact specifications for the design and proportions of the Stars and Stripes. Taft's order was directed primarily at the civil branches of government, since the military already had specs for the flag. The two main points of Taft's order covered the placement of the stars in rows, and the proportions of the flag, which were set at 10:19; the "hoist" (or depth) of the flag at 10 feet, the "fly" (or width) of the flag at 19.

Most American flags sold today are typically much shorter than the official ratio mandates, usually 3 feet × 5 feet or 2 feet × 3 feet. "In effect we have an unofficial national flag used by the population," says Whitney Smith. "On the post office and other government buildings you see the long one [essentially a state and military flag] and elsewhere you see the shorter ones. Some countries have a totally different design for those two flags. In Peru, for example, the state flag has a coat of arms on it and the civil flag does not. There are plenty of examples of this, [in nations] such as the United Kingdom, Finland, and Sweden. There's a £500 fine for flying the Union Jack on a private vessel. That's a Royal Navy flag and it's only for use on the prow, never on the stern."

The exact shades of red and blue were set forth in 1934, and flag manufacturers today refer to them as OG Red and OG Blue—the "OG" standing for "Old Glory." (The flag's popular nickname evolved during the Civil War. It refers to a flag owned by Capt. William Driver, of Salem, Massachu-

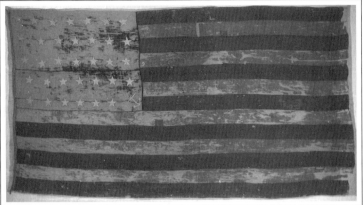

Captain William Driver's flag, Old Glory, famous for flying over
Nashville after its liberation by the North, lent its nickname to
all American flags.

setts. In 1824, Driver's mother and some friends made a twenty-four-star flag as a gift for the merchant captain. The flag sailed around the world twice with Driver and, when he retired, he took it with him to his new home in Nashville, Tennessee. On holidays, Driver would fly the flag he affectionately called Old Glory. In 1860, Driver's wife added some more stars to update the flag, and an anchor was added to the canton to commemorate the captain's seafaring days. The flag became famous when Nashville was liberated by Union troops and Driver's flag was hoisted over the state capitol building. His nickname for the flag had a resonance to it, and soon entered the American lexicon.)

OG Red is a unique color, according to Dale Coots, marketing manager for Annin & Co., America's largest and oldest existing manufacturer of flags. In the standardized color matching system (Pantone) used by modern manufacturers, printers and designers of all kinds, 281C Blue "is pretty much a dead match for OG Blue," says Coots. "The closest to OG Red is 193C Red, but that's a little on the pink side. OG Red is really a blood red with a little blue mixed in."

It took nearly 150 years for the size, design, and colors of the Stars and Stripes to reach something approaching standardization, but while the physical nature of the flag became more defined, its effect on the American psyche became increasingly convoluted.

THE JOHN DIX "shoot-him-on-the-spot" telegraph is legendary for its unequivocal order for action regarding an assault on the flag, but Dix's order was not so much about the flag *per se* as it was about someone trying to seize U.S. property, not to mention that the order was never carried out. There are scores of incidents from the Civil War era in which noncombatants shot—and often killed—each other over the display of flags, both the Stars and Stripes and the Stars and Bars. The benchmark for an irrational act committed in the name of the American flag, however, was set by the U.S. Army in 1862.

In April 1862, Flag Officer David Farragut's force destroyed the Confederate fleet at New Orleans. (Two years later at Mobile, Alabama, Farragut would utter the immortal words, "Damn the torpedoes; Full speed ahead.") Farragut sent a letter to the mayor of New Orleans ordering "that the emblem of the sovereignty of the United States be hoisted over the city hall, mint and custom house by meridian of this day, and all flags and other emblems . . . other than that of the United States, be removed from public buildings at that hour."

Farragut received a reply the following morning, Sunday, April 27. "The city is yours by the power of brutal force," wrote the mayor, "not by my choice or the consent of the inhabitants. As to hoisting any flag not of our own adoption and allegiance . . . the man lives not in our midst whose hand and heart would not be paralyzed at the mere thought of such an act; nor could I find in my entire constituency so desperate and wretched a renegade as would dare to profane with his hand the sacred emblems of aspirations." In other words, the mayor told Farragut to raise his own damned flag. Farragut did just that, ordering the commander of the *Pensacola*, Capt. Morris, to raise the Stars and Stripes over the mint and in sight of his ship. The leader of the crew who raised the flag warned civilian onlookers that the ship would fire on the building if anyone dared mess with the flag. Just a few hours later, the crew of the *Pensacola* was on deck for a joint prayer when four men were spotted tearing down the Stars and Stripes on top of the mint.

The four rabblerousers made no attempt to conceal their identity. The local newspaper reported their names, and recounted that, led by a surly character named William Mumford, they "distinguished themselves by gallantly tearing down the flag that had been surreptitiously hoisted." Mumford and company dragged the Stars and Stripes through the muddy streets, accompanied by the delirious shouts of a mob, and then tore the banner to shreds. Farragut was steamed, and he sent another note to the mayor telling him he had 48 hours to clear the city of women and children. The implication was clear: When time ran out, Farragut's guns would unload on New Orleans. Before that, however, a detachment of marines marched into town and lowered rebel flags from the mint and custom house, replacing them with the Stars and Stripes. On May 1, the army took over for Farragut, under the command of General Butler. Mumford was unfazed by the presence of Billy Yank in his town; an inveterate gambler and braggart, he sought to entertain a crowd in front of the St. Charles Hotel one day by regaling them with his exploits atop the mint. This was folly in many ways, most notably that the hotel was serving as Butler's headquarters. The general had Mumford arrested, and on June 5, 1862, Butler issued Special Order, No. 10:

William B. Mumford, a citizen of New Orleans, having been convicted before a military commission of treason, and an overt act thereof in tearing down the United States flag from a public building of the United States, for the purpose of inciting other evil-minded persons to further resistance to the laws and arms of the United States, after said flag was placed there by Commodore Farragut, of the United States Navy.

It is ordered that he be executed according to the sentence of the said military commission, on Saturday, June 7th inst., between the hours of eight A.M. and twelve M., under the direction of the provost-marshal of the district of New Orleans; and for doing so, this shall be his sufficient warrant.

It was assumed Mumford would be pardoned. He didn't defend himself at trial and, thinking it was assured and would make them look weak, the city council resolved not to petition for his pardon. Butler wasn't adverse to pardons; around the same time he granted reprieve to six Confederate soldiers who had been ordered shot. But, inexplicably, he saw that the execution of Mumford was carried out. It was the most ludicrous thing ever done in the name of the flag, and President Lincoln relieved Butler of command several months later.

Based on the case of William Mumford alone, it is easy to see how the Stars and Stripes could have been eternally reviled in the southern states. For certain, the flag was widely despised in the Confederacy during the war, but when the shooting stopped the Stars and Stripes were able to strike a conciliatory note to some degree. To some who fought for the South, the respect for the Stars and Stripes never left. In a letter after the war, Confederate General William Wickham wrote to a friend:

> I have often said to those with whom I was on terms of friendship that I never saw the United States flag, even when approaching me in battle, that I did not feel arising those emotions of regard for it that it had been wont to inspire. I have, in like manner, said that one of the most painful sights I had ever seen was on the night of the first battle of Manassas, when I saw an officer trailing the flag in the dust before a regiment of the line.

In Charleston, on May 1, 1865, four thousand African-Americans, most of them children, decorated the graves of slain Union soldiers with flowers and flags, in remembrance and thanks. On April 25 of the following year, women in the town of Columbus, Mississippi, followed suit, decorating the graves of both Union and Confederate men who had died in the struggle. On May 6, in Waterloo, New York, the population did likewise. In 1868, Major General John Logan, the leader of a veteran's organization known as the Grand Army of the Republic, set aside May 30 as a day of memorial. The practice eventually became known as Memorial Day and, in 1971, the federal government declared the day, which had started in the South, a legal holiday.

One veteran of the war, Gilbert Bates from Wisconsin,

disagreed with a fellow veteran who averred that the Stars and Stripes were hated in the South. To prove his point, Bates, thirty-three years old at the time, packed an American flag in his bags and boarded a train to Vicksburg, Mississippi, a city that had been reduced to ruin by the siege conducted by Ulysses Grant. Bates got off the train, put the flag on a staff and carried it on his shoulder. And he began to walk, à la Forrest Gump. In Montgomery, Alabama, a major city and briefly the capital of the Confederacy, a crowd turned out to cheer him on.

Through South Carolina, Bates walked along the path taken by the army of William Tecumseh Sherman on its March to the Sea. He was not menaced in any way. At the border with North Carolina, he was met by a color guard of Confederate veterans. On April 14, the sixth anniversary of the bombardment of Fort Sumter, Bates arrived in Washington. He had walked through southern states carrying the Stars and Stripes for three months.

IN 1680, nearly 250 years before Bates's flag march and the war that inspired it, the Dutch explorers Dankers and Sluyter noted the long-term effect of the first instance of flag desecration in the New World; namely, the exclusion of the St. George's Cross in the canton of the flags used by New Englanders. In 1634, long before the good people of Salem, Massachusetts got around to burning witches, they saw evil in other forms. Roger Williams, the famed Puritan minister, who was one of the first Americans to advocate separation of church and state, was still a year away from being banished from the colony for his radical views. When he got the bum's rush from Massachusetts and founded Rhode Island in 1636, he left behind a legacy in the crossless flag. It was Williams who stirred up a certain Mr. Endicott to deface the flag at Salem: The records of Massachusetts from the time indicate "that the ensigns at Salem had been defaced by Mr. Endicott's cutting out part of the red cross. Roger Williams is accused of having agitated the matter, and therefore accountable for the trouble it occasioned." A series of trials dragged on over the course of a year. When the defendants finally got to state their case, they said the "mutilation complained of was done, not from disloyalty to the flag, but from an entirely conscientious conviction that it was idolatrous to allow it to remain, and that having been given to the King of England by the Pope, it was a relic of the anti-Christ."

The question of the use of a cross on a flag was never fully settled. The question was disputed for years, and flags with the cross still flew from forts and other property of the king. Otherwise, flags *sans* cross were used. For his part in the scandal, Endicott was "judged to be guilty of a great offence, inasmuch as he had with rash indiscretion, and by his sole authority, committed an act giving occasion to the court of England to think ill of them." His sentence: admonition and loss for one year of his right to hold public office. William Mumford should have been so lucky.

What is noteworthy about the Endicott–Williams desecration affair is that it clearly raised a question that was very difficult for community leaders and the people they governed to resolve. Aside from the flag in question, nothing has changed in that regard between then and the current day.

William Henry Harrison started the trend of using the flag to sway public opinion in matters that, strictly speaking, had nothing to do with the Stars and Stripes; it wasn't long before his fellow countrymen in the land of the free and the home of the greedy adopted his tactic in the name of capitalism. In the late 1800s, individual states began putting laws on the books about the use of the American flag and their own state flags, but there were no federal laws regarding the flag. A typical state law at the time frowned upon three things: placing marks or pictures on the flag; using a depiction of it in advertisements; and acting to mutilate, defile, deface, defy, trample upon, or cast contempt upon the flag either by words or act. The enforcement of such laws was at best loose and inconsistent. According to Robert Goldstein, America's leading expert on flag desecration, in his book *Desecrating the American Flag,* "several . . . early prosecutions were thrown out by state courts, often on grounds that cast doubt upon the fundamental wisdom and/or constitutionality of flag desecration laws."

One of the early important cases that a court did rule on was the 1900 *Ruhstrat v. People,* which made its way to the Illinois Supreme Court. At issue was the use of a depiction of the flag on cigar boxes. The Court came down on the side of cigars. According to Goldstein, they declared "that the personal liberty protections of both the state and federal constitutions included the right to pursue an occupation, encompassing the right to advertise a business 'in any legitimate matter,' including the use of pictures. The decision also held that the general police power that authorized the passage of state legislation only extended to laws necessitated by threats to the 'public health, safety, comfort or welfare,' and that no such need authorized the state to 'arbitrarily invade the personal rights and personal liberty' of citizens by forbidding the practice of placing pictures of flags on advertising labels.'" The court said the cigar labels were "harmless," and no more disrespectful to the flag than flying it on a ship. The court also suggested that since the Congress had created the flag, only it could make laws regarding it.

The hullabaloo was just getting started. In 1907, the U.S. Supreme Court upheld a 1905 decision by the Nebraska Supreme Court that found the flag desecration laws in that state to be constitutional. The highest court in the land did not hold back its feelings about the Stars and Stripes. According to Goldstein, "in a decision filled with patriotic oratory, [the U.S. Supreme Court] rejected the suggestion that Congress's failure to ban flag desecration prevented state legislatures from doing so. Banning the commercial use of the flag was held to be aimed at a usage that would 'degrade and cheapen' it and thus reflected a proper state intent to 'encourage love and patriotism' among its people." The case was strictly about use of the flag in advertising, but the court opened the door for laws that prevented desecrating the flag to express political dissent. If it was okay for the states to encourage love and patriotism by protecting the flag, it was clear, according to the court, that the same emotions "will diminish in proportion as respect for the flag is weakened."

The question of an individual's right to use the flag in a freely chosen manner became a contentious national issue as America crept closer to involvement in the Great War that exploded in Europe in 1914.

No one knows the identity of the first person in history who decided to burn a flag to make a point; whoever it was knew what he or she was doing. If outrage and anger are the desired results, the most surefire way of eliciting those feelings from an American is to put flame to flag. "What do people do abroad when they want to show opposition to the United States?" poses Whitney Smith. "Across the board, they burn our flag. They know it bends us out of shape to see our flag attacked. Now, if you went to them and said, 'You know, buddy, that's what we do in America when we disagree with the government. You can't burn your own national flag because you'd go to jail. You can burn ours because your government wants you to be anti-American.' That's too sophisticated for them to grasp, though. They know they'll get a knee-jerk reaction and that's all they want."

The first American citizen to be prosecuted for burning the American flag was a man named Bouck White, pastor of the Church of Social Revolution in New York, in 1916. Awaiting trial for desecrating the flag by using it in a cartoon that showed it entangled with money and war, White wasn't about to cave in and, the day before his trial, he burned an American flag. White was found guilty of two separate acts of flag desecration under New York law—one for the cartoon and one for torching the Stars and Stripes. He was fined $100 for each and spent a total of sixty days in the slammer.

Woodrow Wilson, as decent a man who ever sat in the Oval Office, was elected to a second term in 1916 with the help of the popular slogan "He Kept Us Out of War," but to continue to keep the country out of the war was impossible; the German use of torpedoes fired from U-boats at ships of nonbelligerents struck Americans as dirty pool. On April 6, 1917, American doughboys were committed to the trenches of Belgium and France to join British Tommies and French *poilu* in the bloodletting to keep the world, as Wilson put it, "safe for democracy." American citizens had been edgy for some time as the scope of the war in Europe reached across the Atlantic. On January 3, 1917, one of the biggest stories in America was the action taken by L. H. Luksich, a Coast Guard recruiter who worked in New York. On that day, a fellow made the mistake of wiping his muddy hands on the flag at the recruiting center, while Luksich looked on. Luksich responded reflexively; he knocked the offending man on his ass. The story took on greater appeal when it was learned that Luksich was not a native-born American—he was a naturalized citizen from Austria. The Treasury Department was duly impressed and sent Luksich an official commendation for his putting up his dukes to defend the flag. The letter, from Assistant Secretary A. J. Peters, read, in part:

> The department desires to commend you for the spirit of loyalty and patriotism which impelled your ready defense of the national colors, and in voicing this commendation I am not unmindful that you are a naturalized American citizen, for the reason that the incident is rendered the more conspicuous by this fact, and affords gratifying evidence of your assimilation of the spirit and best traditions of the country of your adoption.

The folk-hero status accorded Luksich, though, was an exception among naturalized citizens, aliens, and even native-born Americans of German and Austrian ancestry. On April 2, 1917, in Albany, New York, brewery workers chipped in to buy an American flag and raised it over the beer factory. They formed up in something resembling a military assembly and saluted the flag. One of the group noticed an Austrian coworker idling nearby "with a look of contempt on his face." The group charged after the man, who ran inside and sought shelter in the manager's office. The workers mobbed outside the manager's office brandishing metal spikes and even a little brass cannon they had on hand to salute the flag; they informed the manager that no work would be done until he gave up the Austrian, presumably so he could be beaten to a pulp. The manager did not surrender the man; instead, he fired him and sent him on his way.

Three days later in Paterson, New Jersey, workers at the Cedar Cliff Silk Company mill told the boss they would strike until the Stars and Stripes flew over their workplace. The foreman, John Ulrich, complained that the only flag the company owned was flying at the home office at 752 Broadway in New York. The workers told Ulrich to send someone to get it, and if the flag wasn't up by 1:00 P.M. they were going home. The messenger returned with the flag at 1:10 P.M., but the workers had all departed. The flag was raised, and they returned the next morning.

On the evening of April 6, the day Wilson asked Congress to declare war on Germany, a melee broke out at Rector's, a Manhattan restaurant, when three diners, two of them women, stayed seated while "The Star-Spangled Banner" was played. The song was not yet officially the national anthem, but the assembled at Rector's restaurant didn't care. They surrounded the table of Frederick Boyd, a writer for a socialist newspaper, and Jessie Ashley and May Towle, both lawyers and active suffragists. Punches started flying; while Boyd yelled out that he was English and therefore not required to stand for the song, the women defended themselves with their fists. Boyd was hauled off to night court where he again repeated his claim that he did not have to stand for the song. The judge, Magistrate Corrigan, agreed with him but said that not to do so "was neither prudent nor courteous during these tense times." Boyd was found guilty of disorderly conduct and released with a suspended sentence.

The same day in Trenton, New Jersey, Philip Madino, a Mexican, was sent to the workhouse for six months for spitting on the American flag.

The incident at Rector's did not escape the eye of an anonymous writer in the *Times* Sunday edition on April 8. In a short piece, entitled "Why I Never Rise," he wrote:

> I am the man who always keeps his seat when they play the "The Star-Spangled Banner" in the theatres. You've no doubt noticed me. You've sent ocular daggers at me. Your brain has spat on me. You wanted to black my eye. You thought I was a German spy.
>
> And after you sat down, you kept "rubbering" around at me—all of you. I became a fascinating being immediately. I became a mystery. Your anger having cooled, speculation took possession of your mind—such as it is. Curiosity took the place of anger.

Then you began to pity me. Maybe I was ill. Maybe I had a dear one dead on the western or eastern front. Maybe I was a sincere Socialist or a respectable anarchist who did not believe in bombs or flags. Finally you gave me up and went home to your beer and lobster pâtés.

Well, now, I love the old flag just as much as any of you. And I always keep my seat when it is played, first of all because I like to tease you; and secondly because I fought for it in Cuba and the Philippines, and have only one leg. The other is somewhere in Mindanao.

Whoever penned the letter was one cool customer, but he was part of a tiny minority that would not bow to patriotic convention. On April 9, the Department of Justice released the following warning:

Any alien enemy tearing down, mutilating, abusing or desecrating the United States flag in any way will be regarded as a danger to the public peace or safety within the meaning of Regulation 12 of the proclamation of the President issued on April 6, 1917, and will be subject to summary arrest and confinement.

The very next day, Louis Stoltz of Staten Island, New York, was sent to jail for twenty days, simply because he "used profane language in reference to the American colors."

Stoltz, born in America and a four-year army veteran, denied the charge to no avail; he was of German descent. On April 14, a Slav named Joseph Braick was arrested in Dunellen, New Jersey, for allegedly shredding the Stars and Stripes and stomping on the pieces. Such episodes were so frequent that the District Attorney of New York was bombarded with complaints. The D.A., named Swann, issued a statement on April 20 that said, "In such times as the present when the spirit of patriotism is everywhere apparent, such a law should not be construed too technically. I will not interfere with any proper use of the flag." Swann went on to say, however, that "the man who desecrates the flag by printing an advertisement on it will, of course, be prosecuted." It leaves one to wonder what the lawman meant by "not too technical."

The rage regarding the flag was not limited to spitting aliens. Francis Gilbert, of New York, wrote to the *Times* to remind apparel manufacturers that putting the flag on clothes was a no-no:

> In yesterday morning's issue of your paper you call attention to the fact that various articles of wearing apparel are now being sold with various combinations of red, white and blue affixed thereto, and the paragraph includes the following statement:
>
> "Small American and French flags crossed are also shown on white hose."
>
> . . . I think it might be well to call attention of the trade to this situation. While it may be that the manufacturer of articles of wearing apparel with the flag attached thereto may be prompted by patriotic

motives, yet the sale of such merchandise is clearly in violation of the law.

It was bad enough that some ninnies were walking around with American flags on their socks; in response to what he considered an epidemic of flag desecration, *Times* reader George Soper excoriated the entire metropolis in the Sunday edition on April 20, six years before there was any federal or state flag code suggesting proper etiquette for display of the flag.

> How are we to excuse the abuse of the flag which we see every day in this town? The flag is abused in many ways . . . It is widely used for advertising purposes, being draped about signs announcing auctions, bargain sales, lofts to let, so-called automobile opportunities, shoes, corsets, candles, cameras, imitation jewelry, gum, lager beer, fishing tackle and many other things not ordinarily associated with patriotic sentiment. Show windows are draped and festooned with the colors with no other apparent object than to make shrewd business use of the responsive feelings which are thus aroused. Theatres, especially those which make specialty of the more flashy productions, introduce the flag to extract applause for mediocre dances and melodramatic situations which otherwise would fail to arouse any enthusiasm. Is this patriotic . . . ? [George M. Cohan himself said, "Many a bum show has been saved by the flag."]

There are those who would question whether it is patriotism to carelessly hang Old Glory from the window ledges, often wrong side out, and leave it there untended . . . until the winds have nearly swept it away or wound it into a tangle. It is often painful to see the noble banner in such situations writhing and struggling to be free . . .

By all means see that the flag flies free and is not fouled—if this is not possible, take it in temporarily . . . the most humiliating sight . . . in this city today is the dirty flag which is allowed to thrash itself to pieces above one of the National Guard armories.

. . . Do not hang the flag from a window ledge or balcony. If you must hang it down the side of your building, do not let it remain there too long. Never crowd it into a space too small for it, or display it from your motor car, or buttonhole . . . never let it touch the ground. It is an appropriate and beautiful means of decoration for the hall in which a public meeting for patriotic purposes is to be held, but after the meeting it should be taken down.

Do not display the national flag in front of your house except on patriotic occasions. It means something to your neighbors to see you bring it out; the sight quickens the blood and rouses within every American an inward, if not audible, cheer. It means little that is credible to its owner to see the flag day after day neglected, bedraggled, begrimed, and virtually forgotten . . . Preserve and protect your flag as you would preserve the noble sentiment which it represents.

The dark side of the World War I flagmania in America culminated in 1918 in an episode in flag history that is second only to Mumford's hanging in terms of banner-inspired idiocy. In Montana, a mob surrounded a man named E.V. Starr and demanded that he kiss the flag to make nice after he said the Stars and Stripes were "nothing but a piece of cotton" covered with "a little paint and some other marks." Starr refused to kiss the flag, saying it "might be covered with microbes." A Montana court fined Starr $500 and sentenced him to ten to twenty *years* in the clink. According to Goldstein, a federal judge in the state "termed the sentence 'horrifying'" and one "that justified George Bernard Shaw's comment that American courts had gone 'stark, staring, raving mad' during the war." The federal judge, George Bourquin, took the mob who assaulted Starr to task, calling them "heresy hunters" and "witch burners." Despite this, Bourquin finished up by stating that based on the Supreme Court's upholding of the 1907 Nebraska decision, he was powerless to intervene on Starr's behalf. Starr went to jail.

USING THE IMAGE of the flag to make a buck was prevalent enough in the late 1800s that flag statutes, like the one that sent Starr to jail, started appearing on the books. That some might literally use the Stars and Stripes for profiteering was something that seemed not only unconscionable but downright dastardly. On July 26, 1917, the Federal Trade Commission (FTC) asked Congress to immediately begin debate on new laws that would protect the people from "indefensible" and "extortionate" prices, which the commission alleged were being charged for some commodities since America's entry into the war. The industry that the FTC had in its crosshairs was flag manufacturing. The commission's statement read, in part: "The demand and price situation existing as to flags is typical of a condition caused by the war. Unlawful agencies and acts contemplated by anti-trust laws are not necessary to bring about hardship to the public and the industries of the nation."

The report, signed off on by every member of the FTC, continued:

> The prices of American flags charged by leading manufacturers have increased 100 to 150 percent since April 1916. Scores of others, not regularly engaged in the manufacture of flags, but who are now so engaged, have secured during April and May, 1917, prices ranging from 100 to 500 percent higher than the prices current in April 1916. On high grade display flags the gross profits of the regularly established flag manufacturers on new business done in April and May, 1917, have been 75 to 100 percent, based on the average cost . . . Flags are sold generally by manufacturers direct to retailers, and these, of whom many have themselves paid excessive prices to manufacturers, have secured from the public prices 100 to 300 percent higher than prevailing retail prices of a year ago.

> The total amount of money spent for flags at normal prices is about $5,000,000 each year. Of this amount probably not more than $500,000 has represented the gross profits to manufacturers. But in view

of the recent great increase in demand and volume of sales at abnormally high prices the total profits received by manufacturers are not less than ten times the amount secured during 1916.

The Flagmakers' Association responded by saying that it wasn't their fault; rather, Uncle Sam was to blame. "There are two mills in the United States which supply all of the wool bunting now used in flag manufacture," said one flagmaker. "The government has bought about two-thirds of the bunting for the manufacture of battle flags for army and navy and for signal flags. We used to get a roll of bunting for $5, now that roll costs $15 or $16 . . . When war was declared in April, everybody wanted a flag, and a lot of people went to making flags on an unlimited profit who had never made a flag before. Cloak and suitmakers, and those in the waist trade, started making flags. People would pay anything, and so they charged them anything." The Flagmakers' Association, said its president Spencer Turner, was designed "to promote good fellowship, not to do anything to restrain trade or fix prices."

Curiously, the price of flags quickly began to drop. Good fellowship, that.

PETTY ACTS by small parts of the populace and enforcement of desecration laws aside, the American flag did yeoman's work during World War I. When war was declared against Germany, Boy Scouts rushed down Broadway in New York carrying large versions of the Stars and Stripes.

One newspaper carried a photograph of a Yank soldier at the train depot, his little child holding a flag over the caption, "Will he come home?" Posters to sell war bonds featured a drawing of a weary and bloodied doughboy clutching a flag: OVER THE TOP FOR YOU read the poster, referring to the phrase used by commanders in the trenches at the start of an assault. BUY U.S. GOV'T BONDS, the poster admonished. The bond drives were referred to as "Liberty Loans," and these images were among thousands of the flag used to inspire the home front, just as Norman Rockwell's Rosie the Riveter would during World War II. The flag's most important role during the war, however, was not domestic; for the first time, America's fighting men went "over there" to aid in a fight of European making—the New World headed to the aid of the Old, and tipped the balance in favor of the Allies.

In the years since the two World Wars, it has increasingly become the norm for the rest of the world to adopt a what-have-you-done-for-us-lately attitude toward the United States. This is true to some degree even in Great Britain and France, the two countries that benefited most from American blood in those wars. (This is not to say that America did not benefit from the blood of the young men of those countries.) There is nothing ungrateful about current-day attitudes toward the United States, they are simply a reflection of the mercurial nature of people and the fact that even as those events altered the course of civilization, they occurred a long time ago. Still, on the part of the young men who were plucked from America's cities, small towns, and farms, the willingness to fight in Europe was one of the most monumentally unselfish acts in world history; the people of the besieged nations of Europe certainly felt that way in 1917, and they expressed it in their feelings for the Stars and Stripes.

On April 16, 1917, just ten days after America entered the war, the *New York Times* correspondent in Paris cabled the following short piece:

> In the early hours of this morning there was an unwonted stir in the streets of Paris. Mingled with the sounds of tramping feet choruses of young voices sang blithely in the radiant morning sunshine as the class of 1918—the fourth class of young recruits called up since the war—marched to the stations to leave for the training depots. Crowds of relatives and friends accompanied them laden with hampers and parcels. For all the world they might have been setting out for a fete day so joyful were all faces.
>
> Every class has gone forth bravely, but it was noticeable that none left with such glad expectancy, and that the leavetakings were never before so little fraught with pain. These young men know they are setting out for victory, and as a symbol of this certitude—and perhaps also by way of explanation of it— they wore on their coats and hats the Stars and Stripes, side by side with the tricolor of France.

The American flag flew for the first time over a fighting unit at the front when the Lafayette Escadrille, a squadron of American volunteer fighter pilots who had been fighting alongside French pilots long before the U.S. entered the war, received their official Stars and Stripes from Washington. On

July 8, 1917, the flag was raised, and during the playing of the "Star-Spangled Banner," the chief of the French air services ordered the flags of the French Aviation and Balloon Corps raised on either side of the American banner, symbolically placing them under the protection of Old Glory. The American fliers, in violation of the flag desecration laws in their home states, added the words *Verdun, Somme,* and *Aisne* to represent three mammoth battles during which they patrolled the skies.

In France at the time, it was customary for mothers to hang images of saints and sacred emblems around the necks of their children to keep them safe. In August 1917, Edith Barnard Delano, of East Orange, New Jersey, wrote to the *New York Times:*

> I believe that many of your readers have been as much touched by the reports of the French children kneeling in the streets of Paris as our flag and soldiers passed . . .
>
> A few weeks ago, we enclosed in a letter to a six-year-old daughter of a French poilu who gave his life for France at the Aisne a tiny silk American flag . . .
>
> Today I have the child's reply . . .
>
> "I begged my mother to put the little flag around my neck, and so now I have the flag always with me, and mamma cried for joy and I did too, and I wish the war would end right away."

From Great Britain, the mayor of a small English town wrote to a cousin in America, in February 1918:

Yesterday, for the first time in our history (and I am the 575th Mayor) the flag of the United States flew on this building—and so generally throughout the country. So, though it is more than twenty years since we met, it has brought your name before me. This is no small matter. We look on it chiefly as a justification of our national action in this war. You may take it that, generally speaking, we have wondered at you, and been profoundly sorry for any of your citizens on this side, (that is, when we had time to think about it at all). We knew that, broadly speaking, your notions of right and wrong—of government and civilization—and of decent conduct were the same as ours, and we could not understand how it was that you and your rulers seemed so coldly detached.

And now you have fallen into line and have discovered that unless the German idea of proper human conduct is demonstrated to be false, life on this earth is impossible to any who hold the notions that you and we do of God and humanity. . . . Although we mean to stick to it until we win, the strain and our losses are pretty bad, and as your coming in is bound to shorten things, we are very pleased to greet you.

On July 3, 1918, *New York Times* correspondent Charles A. Selden filed his story on the preparations in Paris to celebrate the Fourth of July:

. . . In Paris the red, white and blue of France is so blended with the red, white and blue of America that it is difficult to tell at a glance where one flag begins and the other ends . . .

The walls of the Louvre, which has looked very gray and grim with locked doors and treasures since the beginning of the war, are now ablaze with the colors of the two Republics, and the black mourning which has draped the statue of the city of Strassbourg in the Place de la Concorde since 1870 when the Germans took Alsace-Lorraine, is relieved by the red, white and blue of America . . .

For several days I had been hearing speeches in the Chamber of Deputies and the Municipal Court about celebrating July 4 in France. They were by no means perfunctory, but they were formal, oratory and official, which never hits you so hard as what Tom, Dick and Harry says and thinks. I wanted to hear what Jean and Francois had to say. I met a small boy with an American flag pinned to the front of his cap and asked him why it was there.

"America," he replied. "My father is a soldier. All the Americans are soldiers, too."

He said it with a splendid air of conviction and finality. No other reason was needed by that boy for wearing an American flag.

. . . I found it [the American flag] there in regions where English will never be spoken. I found it waving in obscure little streets that were streets long before America was discovered, in streets of old Paris, of the Franks and the Romans. It is in streets so narrow that a flag of regulation regimental size could not

At the close of World War I, the Stars and Stripes were in evidence throughout France, particularly in the jubilant streets of Paris.

be suspended across them without its edges brushing against the ancient walls on either side. The beautifully carved stone gateway of the Hotel de Clauny is surmounted by American flags. The Hotel de Clauny, just as it stands today, was finished years before America was discovered . . . Somebody has placed the Stars and Stripes in the ivy growing over the walls of the thermal baths at Cluny, and they date from the first century . . .

I asked a woman standing upon a chair to drape a flag over her door [why she was doing so].

"It is the flag of those who have come," she replied.

. . . On the bank of the Seine in the shadows of Notre Dame [there was a woman]. She was at the edge of the river where the women of that quarter go to do their washing, to quilt and knit and gossip. She had the quilting frame placed horizontally across the backs of two old chairs and was converting whatever she may have started into a big American flag. Over the ground work of the quilt she had sewn seven red and six white stripes, using a small American flag beside her as a model.

In a corner she had stitched a big square of blue and was hurriedly sewing on white stars which a little girl was cutting out for her by means of a paper pattern.

I ran down the steps from the bridge to ask her why.

"Americans," she replied. "I am making a big flag to put across our street tomorrow."

And as she referred to her street she pointed to a tiny, ancient thoroughfare, the Rue St. Julien le Pauvre, which runs down to the quai directly opposite Notre Dame. Somehow, time and history and chronology seemed to reverse themselves as I watched the sewing on the stars and the brick house on Arch Street, Philadelphia, where Betsy Ross made that first American flag, became the ancient place and the quilting woman by the Seine was in a new land.

6

RED LIBBY was a cowboy. He was born in 1892 in a small town in Colorado, and spent most of his early life working with horses and cattle. In the summer of 1914, he was wandering with a buddy through Calgary in the Canadian southwest when, for no reason other than wanting to see the world, he enlisted in the Canadian Army. By 1915, he was in France driving a truck and a short time later he was flying with Britain's Royal Flying Corps. Few, if any, Americans made it to France sooner than Libby. His motive, initially, was not altruistic, and it cost him his standing as a citizen of the United States (though it was later restored). Libby's first flying assignment was as an observer in a two-man craft known as the F.E. 2B (the F.E. stood for Farman Experimental), the ugliest duckling ever to lift off into combat. When he wasn't observing, Libby was firing one of two Lewis machine guns on the ship—one was on a swivel in his little perch at the front of the plane (the propeller was behind the pilot) and the other mounted on the top wing of the bi-plane, which required him to stand up, precariously hanging on to a single steel rod with one hand while firing with the other over the whirring propeller to defend against attacks from the rear. Libby was a crack shot with the machine gun and, by the end of the war, had brought down twenty-two German planes in the service of His Majesty King George V, who awarded him the Military Cross.

In May 1917, one of his British squadron mates came back from leave with two gifts for Libby: a pair of boots and a large American flag. By this time, Libby was one of his group's best pilots and often flew lead or second lead, a position that was marked with either two streamers fluttering from his plane when leading or a single streamer when in second position, since radio contact between planes in a formation did not yet exist. Libby's British commander suggested that Libby use parts of the flag as his leadership streamers. In his war memoirs, *Horses Don't Fly,* Libby wrote, "This was not done with any idea of a stunt to be the first in anything. It was in the line of duty and at the suggestion of my squadron commander, Major Dore." The streamers were the first bits of Stars and Stripes to fly over German lines.

As the war wound to its conclusion, the tattered streamers that flew on Libby's plane were reassembled into something resembling a flag and sent to New York to be auctioned off at a Liberty Loan Drive in October 1918. A *New York Tribune* writer described the scene at Carnegie Hall:

A timid young officer with a tattered thing in his hand mounted the Liberty Theater platform yesterday afternoon, and while he stood there, cheeks burning with embarrassed red, and eyes looking straight down his nose, a crowd that the moment before had gaped and grinned, after one slow stare with a sudden passion, stormed toward him. They rolled forward in a tumult of noise, men and women with welcome in their voices and tears in their eyes. Not Fifth Avenue sightseers cheering a show, but a people greeting their own hero. Then a girl reached out and over the crowd, caught hold of the tattered thing, held it hard and with swimming eyes raised it to her lips. The voices stopped and the air was silent as a prayer. The first American flag to fly over German lines, in the hands of the aviator who carried it there, had come back to New York to be baptized with tears and kisses of a motley New York throng. Those hundreds sought to grasp the precious stripes of red and white and to shake the hand of Captain Frederick Libby. This torn old thing amid all the flags of Fifth Avenue was a holy banner. And so the procession passed along, touching its rags as though becoming a sacrament. Some touched it lightly, some shook it as if it were a paw. The women kissed it, the soldiers saluted it. While Captain Libby still tried to hide behind it with the shame that every real hero seems to have for his own valor.

The National Bank of Commerce paid $3.25 *million* for Libby's flag.

• • •

THE REACTION OF the people at Carnegie Hall to Libby's flag—and the money paid for it—indicate the profound sense of adhesion Americans felt toward the Stars and Stripes. For a symbol of such magnitude, the American flag had, to that point, very few formal or official traditions and ceremonies attached to it; after World War I and during World War II, that changed.

The area of greatest confusion in the use of the banner was with regard to flag etiquette. Some viewed the flag as sacred and worthy of treatment with kid gloves, while others wanted to stick it in their buttonholes and attach it to their automobiles. "There were a lot of flags being used during and directly after World War I," says Whitney Smith. "A lot of people thought it was being used improperly. The army and navy had regulations regarding the flag because they have rules and regulations for everything. Various veterans' organizations had their own ideas, so after the war they all decided to get their act together."

In 1923, the National Flag Conference, made up of sixty-six various groups (including the Ku Klux Klan) agreed on a National Flag Code, based largely on the military's regulations for the flag. Once the code was drawn up, it was printed in pamphlet form and distributed among the masses; even though the Flag Code was not officially adopted by Congress until 1942, its existence was widely known and considered the standard for flag etiquette. "The Flag Code is not a law," says Smith. "It's a resolution of Congress. It has no force of law; you can't break the Flag Code in the sense of breaking the law. On the other hand, if you want to use the flag properly, the Code tells you how. I'm constantly asked by people if it's okay to do this or that thing because it goes against the Flag Code. I say, 'It's legal, but it's not right.' There's a difference."

If the current Flag Code (it has been revised several times) had the power of law, millions of Americans would be violating it, particularly because it covers not only entire American flags, but any "picture or representation . . . upon which will be shown the colors, the stars and the stripes, in any number thereof, or any part or parts of either, by which the average person seeing the same without deliberation may believe the same to represent the flag, colors, standard, or ensign of the United States of America." A handful of examples from the code prove this point:

- The flag should never touch anything beneath it, such as the ground, the floor, water, or merchandise.

- The flag should never be carried flat or horizontally, but always aloft and free.

- The flag should never be used as wearing apparel, bedding, or drapery. It should never be festooned or drawn back, nor up in folds, but always allowed to fall free. (A regulation that came too late for John Wilkes Booth.)

- The flag should never be used for advertising purposes in any manner whatsoever. It should not be embroidered on such articles as cushions and handkerchiefs and the like, printed or otherwise impressed on paper napkins or boxes or anything that is designed for temporary use and discard. Advertising signs should not be fastened to a staff or halyard from which the flag is flown.

- No part of the flag should ever be used as a costume or athletic uniform. However, a flag patch may be affixed to the uniform of military personnel, firemen, policemen, and members of patriotic organizations.

- The flag should not be draped over the hood, top, sides, or back of a vehicle or of a railroad train or boat. When the flag is displayed on a motorcar, the staff shall be fixed firmly to the chassis or clamped to the right fender.

Very few people are cognizant of more than a fraction of the Flag Code; it is very lengthy and, even if its guidelines were enforceable by law, officers would not bother to learn it verbatim. The fact that people *are* aware of slivers of the code has led to widespread and sometimes amusing beliefs, though. For instance, many people are convinced that if an American flag touches the ground it must be burned. "That's a classic," says Smith with a grin. "I like to tell people that in the more liberal states it's allowed to touch the ground three times before you have to burn it." This false belief is likely born of mixing up two elements of the Flag Code: that the flag shouldn't touch the ground, and that burning the flag is the recommended way to dispose of one that is worn out. The code says a worn out flag should be "destroyed in a dignified way, preferably by burning." No other helpful hints for disposal are included, and it's odd that the only recommended way of getting rid of a flag is the same method used by people to infuriate flag devotees.

Some other legends are also derived in part from the Flag Code. One of the more famous is that the flag is not dipped in deference to foreign leaders when a U.S. Olympic team marches the flag into a stadium away from our shores. The code clearly states that "the flag should not be dipped to any person or thing," but the code did not exist when the practice is alleged to have started. The story goes that, among the 1908 U.S. Olympic team that went to London, there was a disproportionate number of Bostonians, i.e., a lot of descendants of Ireland. The night before the ceremonies, they drank beer and cursed the King. One of them suggested it would be a real kiss off to the King if the flag was not dipped before him the following day. However, this is nothing more than a popular myth: A *New York Times* reporter traveling with the American team reported upon leaving America that "It would be impossible to bring together a more cosmopolitan team. There are two Indians and two negroes, and many of Irish or German origin. I have noticed the colors of nearly all the principal colleges—Yale, Harvard, Princeton, Cornell, University of Pennsylvania, Columbia, Michigan, Chicago, Dartmouth, Marquette, University of Illinois and of Virginia."

Moreover, *The Times* of London reported exhaustively on the opening ceremony the following day, July 14, 1908.

> . . . Then came the English-speaking races, headed by the Stars and Stripes, with Canada, Aus-

tralasia and South Africa following, their flags all variants on the Union Jack, placed next to the representatives of the Mother Country . . .

. . . The effect of the procession was to a certain extent marred by the fact that several of the competitors appeared in mufti . . .

. . . The United States representatives, who were preceded by a gentleman in a frock coat and top hat, were wearing ordinary clothes and caps with badges, but that did not prevent [them from being] received with shouts of general applause, punctuated by the college yells with which the visits of Harvard and Yale athletes have made us familiar . . .

No scandal there, other than a fashion violation.

In other cases, legends regarding the flag have no link to the Flag Code. The most prevalent of these is that to stand trial in the presence of a flag with fringe around the edges means that you've given up your constitutional rights and subjected yourself to military tribunal law. "Nonsense," says Smith. Fringe on a flag is merely decorative.

Just as people genuinely want the colors of the American flag to mean something specific, they look for specific meaning in customs regarding the flag. Why is the flag folded into a triangle? What does it mean when the flag flies at half-mast? "There is no meaning to the triangle," says Smith. "It's simply a matter of convenience the military came up with. Flying the flag at half-mast just has general meaning; when you're victorious, you fly your flag high. Some think the empty space above a flag at half-mast is for the invisible banner of death—death has conquered all. Others relate it to the fact that on board a ship and in other military situations, a disheveled condition was characteristic of death. Everyone is familiar with the riderless horse with the boots reversed in the stirrups; on ships they used to put all the riggings and sails in disarray, and also the uniforms of the men. As far as specific origin of the flag at half-mast, no one really knows. Unfortunately, with customs, the first person who does something doesn't go home and write it down: 'Today I went to raise the flag, but since someone died it didn't feel right so I lowered it half way.' "

There is no requirement or law that states American flags must be made in America, although most high-quality, embroidered Stars and Stripes are manufactured in the U.S. The federal government buys more than 100,000 American-made Stars and Stripes every year to sell or give away to constituents after they've supposedly flown over the Capitol. To call this a racket would be mild. "The price people pay for them is actually less than wholesale," says Smith, "because the company that gets the contract to make the flags gives the government a fantastic deal. Flag retailers hate this practice: Here's some congressman getting all this favorable publicity—some judge retires or some school teacher is honored—and they give them a flag that 'flew over the Capitol.' Of course, the recipient thinks it's *the* flag that flew over the Capitol. Well, there's a deck out there [at the Capitol building] not visible from the street, and there are six full-time guys who go up there with a stack of boxes filled with flags and they raise 'em up and lower 'em down, fold them and put them back in the box—all in ninety seconds from out of the box to back in. At one point they caught the guys up there not even bothering to take the flags out of the box. Who would know, right? Now they have video cameras to make sure they actually raise the flags, however briefly. A friend of mine likes to joke they could save a lot of time and money by just piling all the flags on Air Force One and making a pass over the Capitol."

The Flag Code includes mention of the Pledge of Allegiance and the manner in which it should be delivered, that is, "rendered by standing at attention facing the flag with the right hand over the heart." Considering the magnitude and number of controversies that have surrounded the Pledge over the years on religious and educational grounds, it is probably the most explosive single run-on sentence known to Americans. It is also one of the silliest, based on its origins.

In 1892, the magazine *Youth's Companion* needed a circulation gambit, a nineteenth-century version of the Publishers Clearing House Sweepstakes. The staff of the magazine had an inspired publicity idea: to celebrate the 400th anniversary of Columbus's famous voyage, they would offer, at cost, American flags to schools so the kids could have a focus to any little ceremony they might concoct. They might get a local Civil War veteran to come in and give a speech, and then could all pledge their allegiance to the flag. To help the idea along, the words to a pledge were written. They were likely written by either Francis Bellamy or James Upham, both of whom worked at the magazine. (The descendants of both men claim credit for their family member, and there is no clear record.) The pledge the school kids in 1892 recited went like this: "I pledge allegiance to my flag and the Republic for which it stands, one nation, indivisible, with liberty and justice for all."

The Congress did not officially recognize the Pledge until 1942, and when they did a minor change was made. For years, when those reciting the Pledge said the words "to my flag" the right hand was removed from the chest and the right arm was extended straight out toward the flag with the palm upturned. "That looked very close to the Nazi salute," says Smith, "so when Congress adopted it they said, 'Let's leave that hand on the chest.'" Two well-known words, "under God," were added to the Pledge by an Act of Congress in 1954. On that occasion, President Dwight Eisenhower remarked of the simple phrase, "In this way we are reaffirming the transcendence of religious faith in America's heritage and future; in this way we shall constantly strengthen those spiritual weapons which forever will be our country's most powerful resource in peace and war." Almost as soon as those words were spoken, many Americans disagreed with them, and many still do today.

The Flag Code recommends that Americans fly the Stars and Stripes on a daily basis from sunrise to sunset. Nighttime flying with illumination got a thumbs-up in 1976, but flying the flag in inclement weather is a breach of the code unless it's made of an all-weather material. For those who aren't everyday flag fliers, the code suggests the flag be displayed on these days: New Year's Day, Inauguration Day (January 20), Lincoln's Birthday (February 12), Washington's Birthday (third Monday in February), Easter Sunday, Mother's Day (third Hallmark store on the right), Armed Forces Day (third Saturday in May), Memorial Day (half-mast until noon, then full staff, on the last Monday in May), Flag Day (June 14), Independence Day, Labor Day (first Monday in September), Constitution Day (September 17), Columbus Day (second Monday in October), Navy Day (October 27), Veterans Day (November 11), Thanksgiving Day, Christmas Day, and the dates states were admitted to the Union and other state holidays. New to the list in 2002 is Patriot Day, September 11, the anniversary of the terrorist attacks on the World Trade Center and the Pentagon, and the crash of a fourth airliner in the countryside of Pennsylvania.

It's an odd list: religious holidays mixed in with military and historic commemorations, and, of all things, Mother's Day. One occasion that stands out on the list, however, is the one dealing with an inanimate object: Flag Day. According to Whitney Smith, the town of Waubeka, Wisconsin, traditionally claims that Flag Day, a birthday celebration of sorts for the flag, originated there in 1885, when a school teacher named Bernard Cigrand held a ceremony in its honor. There are several other people associated with the founding of Flag Day, but Smith believes the first suggestion for honoring the flag came during the Civil War when Dudley Warner, the editor of the Hartford, Connecticut, *Evening Press,* suggested on June 8, 1861, that a day honoring the flag was in order. People responded to Warner's call by flying the Stars and Stripes all over Connecticut. President Woodrow Wilson issued a proclamation establishing June 14 as Flag Day in 1916; the Congress authorized recognition of the day in 1949.

Of all the words ever spoken or written about the American flag, there are none so eloquent as those spoken by Wilson on Flag Day in 1917, just two months after he and the Congress committed the country to war.

> My Fellow Citizens—
>
> We meet to celebrate Flag Day because this flag which we honor and under which we serve is the emblem of our unity, our power, our thought and purpose as a nation. It has no other character than that which we give it from generation to generation. The choices are ours. It floats in majestic silence above the hosts that execute those choices, whether in peace or in war. And yet, though silent, it speaks to us—speaks to us of the past, of the men and women who went before us and of the records they wrote upon it. We celebrate the day of its birth; and from its birth until now it has witnessed a great history, has floated on high the symbol of great events, of a great plan of life worked out by a great people. We are about to carry it into battle, to lift it where it will draw the fire of our enemies. We are about to bid thousands, hundreds of thousands, it may be millions, of our men, the young, the strong, the capable of the nation, to go forth and die beneath it on fields of blood far away—for what? For some unaccustomed thing? For something for which it has never sought the fire before? American armies were never before sent across the seas. Why are they sent now? For some new purpose, for which this great flag has never been carried before, or for some old, familiar heroic purpose for which it has seen

men, its own men, die on every battlefield upon which Americans have borne arms since the Revolution?

These are the questions which must be answered. We are Americans. We in our turn serve America, and can serve her with no private purpose. We must use her flag as she has always used it. We are accountable at the bar of history and must plead in utter frankness what purpose it is we seek to serve . . .

WILSON CHALLENGED the Americans who came after him to give the Stars and Stripes whatever character they would possess at any given moment. This was a tough chore to pass down the line; it's easier to rely on the past to imbue the flag with its magic. If, as Wilson told us, the character of the American flag is inextricably linked to its people, then its character can best be described as manic. At their best, the American people made the flag synonymous with freedom in the twentieth century; at its lowest, the flag assumed the character of conniving, duplicitous holders of high office, who exploited the banner's symbolic weight for their own ends. Often, with the notable exception of the two World Wars, Americans were at odds over their relationship with their flag.

When World War II ended on August 15, 1945, the flag was never more popular. Trying to capture the scene in Times Square, a *New York Times* reporter wrote:

Everywhere noisemakers were in evidence. Automobiles, taxis, trucks ran through the streets with passengers not only inside but on running boards and tonneaux, and even on engine hoods, shouting and blowing horns. Thousands of pedestrians carried small American flags and there was hardly a vehicle that did not display the Stars and Stripes . . .

The war's end, coming at a time when gloom pervaded the city—reports through the late afternoon dealt principally with speculation that the Japanese reply would prove unsatisfactory—sharpened the reaction. It was instantaneous and wild. But beneath the noises, the surface hilarity, could be detected a feeling of deep release.

The flag lowered from the American embassy in Tokyo on the day Japan attacked Pearl Harbor was raised over the Ontario County Court House in Canandaigua, New York. Maps in newspapers showed little flags on top of the bases and cities on Japan's mainland occupied by American forces. When the Japanese signed the surrender document in the presence of Douglas MacArthur onboard the battleship *Missouri* in Tokyo Bay, they did so in front of the very same Stars and Stripes that had flown from the flagship of Matthew Perry's vessel when he opened up Japan in 1853.

Of the countless images of the American flag from the 1770s to the current day, the best known and most popular is a photograph of five marines and a combat medic raising it over Mt. Suribachi, on the Pacific island of Iwo Jima, on February 23, 1945. The moment was captured in a brilliant exposure by Joe Rosenthal of the Associated Press. The photo appeared on the front page of nearly every newspaper

Marines raising the flag on Iwo Jima: Joe Rosenthal's famous photograph is perhaps the most resonant and beloved image of the American flag.

New Yorkers crowd Times Square to celebrate the defeat of
Japan and the end of World War II. Naturally, the Stars and
Stripes are apparent everywhere.

in America and was so perfect that, for years, it was widely considered to be a staged act for propaganda use. It was not; in fact, two flags were raised by the marines on Suribachi that day. The first was very small, and the marines who were still under fire on the beach could not see it. Realizing the morale boost the Stars and Stripes would give the marines down below, a message was passed up the line to raise a larger flag. It was this flag raising—the second one—that Rosenthal got on film. The image was used for everything from war-bond posters to postage stamps, and later served as the model for the Marine Corps War Memorial in Washington, D.C.

On the day of the Japanese surrender, a full page photo of nearly a dozen American flags appeared in the *New York Times,* accompanied by these stirring words:

> *Oh thus be it ever*
> *when freemen shall stand*
> *Between their loved home*
> *and wild war's desolation.*

It was an advertisement for Bloomingdale's.

By the 1960s, advertising had insinuated itself so fully into everyday life that people no longer looked askance at the use of the Stars and Stripes in ads. To use the flag for commercial purposes runs contrary to the Flag Code to this day, but any thought of banning such acts by law lost steam simply because the idea of doing so seemed old-fashioned. According to Goldstein, "in 1966 the National Conference of Commissioners on Uniform State Laws, which in 1917 had recommended that all states enact a Uniform Flag Law . . . withdrew the proposal in its entirety from its list of recommended statutes, on the grounds that it was 'obsolete.' "

Advertisements featuring the Stars and Stripes seemed like small potatoes to flag lovers once the act of setting the flag ablaze as part of political protests became a familiar sight. Flag burning was never a fad; the total number of these torchings in American history is really quite small. It seemed a fad, however, once images of burning flags began appearing in newspapers and on television. When the nation's military involvement in Vietnam grew, so too did discontent. It was America's most unpopular war of the twentieth century—not everyone was against it, but those who were made themselves heard. Flags were burned here and there in 1965 and 1966 but, on April 15, 1967, a flag was lit in Central Park in New York, and so was a bitter controversy. On that day in Central Park, more than 200,000 people took place in an antiwar demonstration, and photos of the burning flag were on front pages across the country the following day. Within a month, a House Judiciary subcommittee was holding hearings on potential federal flag-desecration laws. According to Goldstein, by the time the hearings started on May 8, "more than sixty house members had already proposed virtually identical flag desecration bills, which generally banned a wide variety of acts, such as burning and mutilation," as well as that old standby from the obsolete state flag laws, spoken or written words that "cast contempt upon the flag." During the debate, the people's elected representatives referred to those who burned flags as traitors, misfits, anarchists, rats, crackpots, and irresponsible louts. A bill made its way through the House and the Senate and onto the desk of President Lyndon Johnson, who signed it into law on July 4, 1968. The legislation did not make it illegal to say disparaging things about the flag—this was perceived as too obvious a violation of the First Amendment's guarantee of free speech—but striking the language pertinent to verbal contempt did not have the desired effect of thwarting challenges to the new law.

The number of flag desecration cases during the Vietnam War numbered in the thousands; most were for simple things such as wearing a flag patch on clothing, or, especially popular subjects for photographers and television cameramen, replacing the union of stars on a flag with the peace sign. In most cases, those dragged into court were war protesters or other people who simply looked to be antiestablishment types. According to Goldstein, most were prosecuted under old state statutes rather than the new federal flag law. Decisions were mixed: Guilty verdicts were just as often dismissed by appeals courts as they were upheld. In short, the legal world was in a tizzy over flag desecration and remained so, according to Goldstein, because the U.S. Supreme Court ". . . repeatedly ducked the fundamental issue: whether physical flag destruction used to express political dissent was a form of symbolic speech protected by the First Amendment."

When the Republican National Convention renominated Ronald Reagan in Dallas in 1984, protesters burned an American flag in front of city hall amid a storm of petty vandalism. A slew of people were arrested for disorderly con-

Reuters NewMedia Inc./CORBIS

Burning the American flag in protest is widespread abroad and furiously debated at home, as many still squabble over whether or not flag burning is in fact an expression of speech and therefore protected by the First Amendment.

Bettman/CORBIS

duct, and one of them, Joey Johnson, was detained a bit longer and charged with violating a Texas state law known as the Venerable Objects Law. Johnson was found guilty in the Dallas County Criminal Court and sentenced to one year in jail. The trial was dubious; only one witness, an undercover policeman, fingered Johnson as the flag burner. Even though copious amounts of videotape existed of the incident, none of it showed Johnson burning the flag, and none of it was admitted as evidence. Johnson said he didn't do it, and his lawyers argued that even if he had done it—and they continually asserted he had not—the Texas law violated Johnson's First Amendment rights to do so to make a political statement. The judge, John Hendrik, instructed the jury that under Texas' "law of parties" they could convict Johnson simply for encouraging or aiding others to burn the flag. Assistant Dallas County D.A. Michael Gillett told the jury that Johnson "was guilty as sin as far as the law of parties is concerned," and urged them to hit Johnson with the maximum penalty of a year in prison because he "had offended the nation"; the jury could, said Gillett, "represent each and every American" in delivering a "message" to Johnson and "others like him." That message, said Gillett, was, "No more. We won't have it."

The law allowed Johnson to post a bond and stay out of jail while the case was appealed. An appeals court upheld the decision but was on very thin ice in doing so; the court agreed that flag burning was protected by free speech, but that the state could infringe upon Johnson's constitutional rights because they thought he was a real unsavory character and that his alleged act was so "inherently inflammatory" that the state had to "act to prevent breaches of the public peace." Johnson requested that the Texas Court of Criminal Appeals hear the case. It did, and on April 20, 1988, it ruled 5–4 that the Venerated Objects Law had been abused in Johnson's case and violated his First Amendment rights.

The U.S. Supreme Court had ruled on flag issues before Johnson's case. In 1943, it upheld a decision to ban compulsory flag saluting in public schools, but had to that point avoided entirely the matter of flag desecration. Its days of dodging the controversy were over, however. On October 17, 1988, *Texas v. Johnson* was added to its docket as case No. 88-155. The flag was a hot-button issue at the time because, in his debates with Democratic nominee Michael Dukakis, the soon-to-be-elected George Bush continually chided the Democrat for a veto he'd executed in 1977 as the governor of Massachusetts. The law Dukakis nixed in 1977 would have required public school teachers to lead their students in a daily Pledge of Allegiance. Bush hammered home his point by asking the people, "What is it about the American flag that upsets this man so much?" It was the oldest trick in the book: using the flag to make a political opponent seem a lesser American, and voters ate it up.

The oral arguments before the Supreme Court on March 21, 1989, were unusually heated. Justice Antonin Scalia posed that acts of flag desecration did not make the Stars and Stripes "any less a symbol." Not only that, said Scalia, such acts "would have been useless unless the flag was" already a "very good symbol." Justice Anthony Kennedy thought the Dallas County Assistant D.A., Kathi Drew, was proposing that the court make a "flag exception" to the First Amendment. Drew shot back that the flag was "an important symbol of national unity," that it was public property in which every American had a stake, and, as such, the state was just as interested in avoiding its misuse as it would be in preventing people from "painting swastikas on the Alamo." Scalia was flabbergasted at that suggestion, and got a laugh from the assembled when he said, "I never thought the flag I owned is your flag."

On June 11, 1989, the court decided 5–4 that Texas law was unconstitutionally applied and deprived Johnson of his First Amendment right to peaceful political expression. The case troubled the members of the Supreme Court like few in its history. Kennedy, one of the five who voted in favor of Johnson, wrote a separate concurring opinion in which he said he found the decision-making process "painful" and that it had exacted from him "a personal toll." Nonetheless, continued Kennedy, the constitution required that "we must make decisions we do not like" and that it was "poignant but fundamental that the flag protects those who hold it in contempt."

The four dissenters seemed on the brink of outrage. Chief Justice Rehnquist thought the flag was above the ordinary principles of law, and Justices White and O'Connor agreed with him. Justice Stevens said that "if liberty and equality" were "worth fighting for," then it could not follow that "the flag that uniquely symbolizes their power is not itself worthy of protection from unnecessary desecration." The act of burning the flag, said some of the dissenters, was akin to defacing the Lincoln Memorial.

Polls showed Americans hated the decision. More than

65 percent disagreed with the ruling and 71 percent favored a constitutional amendment to overturn it. Sen. Strom Thurmond, who many reckoned was as old as the flag itself, took to the pulpit and declared: "We must stand up for America! The flag! The flag! America! America, for us!"

To this day, the argument over whether flag desecration is an act unrelated to speech or is, in fact, a form of expression, continues. The proposed amendment to the constitution is a single sentence: "The Congress shall have the power to prohibit the physical desecration of the flag of the United States." As of this writing, the proposed amendment has yet to make it simultaneously through the House and the Senate. In every case, it has been defeated by a mere handful of votes. The amendment's supporters continue to press its case.

ON AUGUST 21, 1959, President Dwight Eisenhower issued the necessary Executive Order to add a single star to the flag to acknowledge Hawaii's entrance into the union of states. That order meant that, on July 4, 1960, the total number of stars on the United States flag had reached fifty, where it remains today, forty-two years later, and for the foreseeable future.

Gone, long ago, are the days when the Stars and Stripes were made one at a time by seamstresses cutting individual stars out of cotton. A quality American flag, however, is still very much a hands-on production. Annin & Co., founded in 1847, America's largest and oldest manufacturer of flags, is headquartered in Roseland, New Jersey, but no flags are made there. The actual manufacturing takes place at several plants around the country, one of which is in the town of Oaks, Pennsylvania. In a typical week at its Oaks plant, Annin employees churn out 25,000 small flags (3 feet × 5 feet or 6 feet × 10 feet) and five hundred big flags (20 feet × 30 feet or 30 feet × 60 feet). The larger flags are frequently purchased by businesses to skirt local ordinances regarding the placement and size of signs. The big flags are attention getters, and no local municipality would be crazy enough to take on the size or placement of the American flag.

Each morning, a truck departs from Oaks to deliver finished flags to Roseland for distribution to flag retailers. Before making the return trip, the truck picks up one hundred 150-yard rolls of OG Red and OG White fabric. The truck then swings by an Annin plant in East Orange, New Jersey, to pick up blue cantons of stars. The cantons for the small flags arrive at Oaks in 60-foot strips consisting of 20 fields of 50 stars. Each strip of 20 is embroidered simultaneously in East Orange—one thousand needles machine-gunning one thousand stars.

The rolls of OG Red and OG White are placed on machines known as *slitters,* which do just what their name implies: They slit the rolls into stripes. After slitting, the 150-yard rolls of fabric are joined into *shorts* and *longs.* A *short* is the series of stripes at the top of the flag. There are seven stripes in a short, the top one is red, as is the bottom one. The *longs* start with a white stripe and end with a red one. Initially, two stripes of red and white are joined. Then a single stripe is added to start a short, or two stripes are attached to start a long. Each bobbin in the automated sewing machines holds 174 yards of thread, enough for an entire roll joined with a lock stitch. Annin prefers the lock stitch to the chain stitch, which resembles the string on a bag of dog food, because once the chain stitch starts to unravel, it won't stop. It takes twelve minutes for an entire roll to work through the sewing machines.

Once joined, the short and long stripes are bundled up, placed on wooden carts called *horses,* and pushed to an area where they are checked by hand for faults. If any are found, they are removed with scissors. At the next stop, the shorts and longs are cut free hand into flag lengths by workers who have been on the job for twelve years, on average. In a process called the *short join,* fields of stars are attached to shorts by feeding them through a sewing machine by hand. Aside from the electric sewing machine, there is nothing automatic about the short join. In the *long join,* the longs are sewn to the now united shorts and fields. If no defects were found along the way, the result is 150 yards of flag. The length of flag descends through a sheet metal chute, fed by electronic sensors to a lower floor, where they are cut and squared by hand. If the corners match up, the flag is square and good to continue on. The fly end of the flag is then sewn with a four-needle fly hem to reinforce it, because the primary cause of flags shredding is their whipping against themselves in the wind. The banding (or heading)—the strip of material on the hoist side of the flag—is attached next. The banding is 1.5 inches and is made of polyester, and once it's applied the flags are put on horses and sent to inspection.

A two-person team inspects the flag and folds it into a square, clearing it for the final steps. A grommet machine takes two pokes at the flag: the first one makes the holes and the subsequent one inserts the brass grommet. The company label is then applied and the flag is packed in a box. Only when the flag is in the box do the employees consider it an American flag; up until then, it's treated as ordinary material.

The area in which large flags are made is a virtual sea of red, white, and blue strewn across the floor, fed into sewing machines by hand. Keeping track of what is being sewn would be impossible for anyone other than a veteran sewer. The stars on large flags are not embroidered, but are appliquéd. They are diecut with adhesive on one side; and the cantons are drilled with holes to indicate placement. Employees take the cantons and stars home with them at night and iron them on; the next day, the stars are sewn on with a zigzag switch. The floor in the large flag unit is measured off and marked in black felt pen so the length of the flags can be gauged. For a 30 feet × 60 feet flag, the floor is marked: 725 inches/60.5 feet. The five extra inches are folded back over and lock-stitched to prevent the damage that would occur from such a gargantuan flag beating itself up. When the flag is finished, a whistle, just like one worn by a basketball referee, is blown. Any seven people who are handy converge on the flag spread out on the floor to help fold it. Once folded, it requires two people to carry it to the grommet machine.

In a given week, about half of Annin's Oaks plant production goes to Roseland for distribution to retailers who specialize in flag sales. The other half are sent to an Annin facility in Ohio for distribution to mass merchandisers, such as Wal-Mart.

"Patriotism goes up and down," says Dale Coots, marketing manager for Annin. "And flag sales go up and down with it."

Beginning in 1999, Annin noticed an unexpected spike in sales. For this, they could thank America's mightiest domestic huckster, Martha Stewart, who featured flags prominently as ideas for home decor in the July/August 1999 issue of her magazine and in the Summer 2000 edition of her catalog, *Martha By Mail.*

The busy season for flag manufacturing runs from mid-March through July 4. By Labor Day, Annin's inventory is at its lowest.

THE FLAG BOOM that occurred after September 11, 2001, was "probably the quickest and most widespread" in U.S. history, according to Whitney Smith. "That's a reflection of the communications systems we have today, and the fact that flag booms are usually associated with significant events. One indication of the size of demand is that almost every manufacturer limited production strictly to American flags."

At Annin & Co., demand for flags in September 2001 was twenty times greater than during a typical September. "More American flags were sold in the ten days following September 11 than in the nine months previous," says Dale Coots. "And you have to keep that in perspective because, in normal times, only 15 percent of the flags we make eventually end up with consumers. The other 85 percent is commercial."

Annin put a moratorium on producing any flags other

than fifty-star American flags. Two of their plants already made only Stars and Stripes, and they shifted capacity at two of their other plants to try to keep up with demand. It was an impossible task. In March 2002, Annin expected that it would have fulfilled its back orders by midsummer.

The September 11 surge in the popularity of the American flag was massive. "People were calling us almost in a panic," says Carolyn Albanese, Annin's head of customer service in Roseland. "They didn't just want to buy flags, they *needed* flags. Many of the calls we got were from consumers who just didn't understand why we didn't have flags. Dealers were telling us they could see the panic on people's faces. We had a guy from the USO in New York drive down. He wanted small flags to hand out to people. We didn't have them. We had a nun in the lobby who wanted a flag and she just wouldn't leave. We thought we were going to have to call the police. Whatever she wanted, we'd have given to her if we had it. But we didn't."

"Our season was over," says Dale Coots. "Our warehouses were nearly empty and we were wiped out. When people couldn't get flags they started showing up at the front door. We had to lock the doors and put a camera in the lobby. They didn't understand that coming here is like showing up at GM and saying you want to buy a car. We didn't have any for the dealers or the public. One of our competitors in the Midwest had to call the local police to keep order in their parking lot."

The first flag boom of the twenty-first century was both touching and freakish: In a single day immediately after September 11, 2001, Wal-Mart stores sold 118,000 Stars and Stripes; television networks and newspapers teamed the flag with logos that read things such as "Attack on America" and "America at War"; every government figure who appeared on television wore an American flag pin; a mother in New York yanked her child from school when teachers failed to follow a Board of Education order to recite the Pledge of Allegiance; a dispute between two independent flag retailers over a wrong address delivery of flags from Annin made its way to the syndicated television show *The People's Court;* key rings, hats, decals and jewelry featured the flag; syndicated comic strips such as "Blondie" and "Family Circus" acknowledged the flag boom ("I'll find your car for you, Mommy," says Jeffy in a parking lot filled with flag-bearing autos. "It has a flag on it."); Hollywood actors appeared on television with the flag as a backdrop to encourage tolerance of Muslim Americans.

One moment, however, trancended them all: three New York firemen raised a flag amid the ruins of the World Trade Center in a moment evocative of Iwo Jima, and Americans cheered the immediately famous—and ubiquitous—image. The flag eventually made its way to the Super Bowl, the Winter Olympics in Salt Lake City, and the Final Four of the NCAA men's basketball championship, and Americans cheered some more.

The sincerely patriotic and the merely opportunistic quickly seized on the flag as the symbol of choice after September 11: within a week of September 11, the television airwaves were crackling with advertisements for the "American Freedom Collection" of flags and decals to affix to automobiles ("Hurry, order now! This $14.99 offer is limited!"); the U.S. Postal Service had one *billion* stamps with the flag on them in post offices by November 1, 2001; volunteer firefighters from Upper Black Eddy, Pennsylvania, a hamlet no bigger than a shoe, rallied other local volunteers and stitched together a 20 foot × 30 foot flag consisting of hundreds of tiny American flags and took it to New York; pizza boxes were printed with the flag and the message, "United We Stand"; finding that message to be a cliché, bumper stickers began to appear reading "We Stand United"; a flag appeared that attempted to cram every possible sentiment onto one banner, including an image of the Stars and Stripes, the Statue of Liberty, and the words, "God Bless America"; Stars and Stripes were fashioned from Christmas-tree lights and glowed through the night; a community college advertised its criminal justice program with the words "Your country needs you" emblazoned over the American flag; Hallmark launched a line of greeting cards with patriotic themes, including one showing the Stars and Stripes and the words, "Courage, Honor, Loyalty"; Wal-Mart sold Little Patriots Diapers, festooned with blue stars; a list of sports betting odds in the New York *Daily News* called itself "America's Line," the words appearing over a silhouette of the United States covered in the Stars and Stripes; the FDNY's Ladder Company 10 took delivery of a new truck painted like an American flag; and army recruiting minivans roamed the streets of America made up like flags with windows, bumpers and all.

Meanwhile, at Annin, the job became more than just a job. "This may sound corny," says Carolyn Albanese, "but I work at a company that makes the United States flag. I felt like we had a chance to help people heal by getting them their flags and answering the phones instead of turning on answering machines. I think the people who work here feel passionate about it; it's not just a product. It feels special to give people something that gives them a sense of security and tells them everything is going to be okay."

THE POST–SEPTEMBER 11 surge in patriotism and display of the Stars and Stripes was welcomed and embraced by the people at large but, in some quarters, the boom had a nauseating effect. Newspaper editorial writers were freaked out by it; Maureen Dowd of the *New York Times,* for example, thought President George W. Bush was "playing the flag card." In the same paper's Sunday magazine, writer George Packer said the flag wouldn't fly at his home because he thought to display the Stars and Stripes "wasn't just politically suspect, it was simply bad taste, sentimental, primitive . . ." Norman Mailer, apparently still alive and miserable, whined to the British newspaper *The Daily Telegraph,* "Has there ever been a big powerful country that is as patriotic as America? And patriotic in the tinniest way, with so much flag-waving?" E. R. Shipp, in New York's *Daily News,* wrote: "We do appear to be going overboard. I do believe in places like Long Island people are trying to outdo their neighbors for dramatic display of the flag." *The Philadelphia Inquirer* chimed in with its headline: "Does flag-waving signal U.S. chauvinism? Some Americans fear the line between patriotism and belligerence may blur." If by "some Americans" they meant newspaper writers, academics, and showbiz types, the headline writers were spot on. The comic strip "Doonesbury" spoke for those who felt the political right had absconded with the American flag many moons ago. "You guys hijacked the flag years ago during the Cold War, especially the Vietnam Era, turning it into a symbol of unquestioning, jingoistic nationalism. Now it's back to being a symbol of patriotism and love of country, not a particular political agenda! So thanks for restoring it to all of us!"

THE BREADTH OF emotion that surged along with the American flag after September 11, 2001, proved that one way or another, the flag means something to every American. What follows are the thoughts of five Americans whose connection with the flag is more intimate than simply hanging it from a car window.

Margaret M. Malone was born in 1919, in Long Island City, New York. Today she lives in Hamilton Square, New Jersey, and remains active in the Mercer County Women's Post of the American Legion #447. She serves on the Legion's National Legislative Council. On September 11, 2001, she was in Washington, D.C., on Capitol Hill for a meeting with the Joint Senate and House Committee on Veteran Affairs. One of the topics slated for discussion was the flag desecration amendment.

I joined the WACs in 1943. You had to be alive then to understand the feeling. My husband, Ray, served in North Africa and Italy. He was an observer on a Catalina scout plane. He got hurt in a crash and they sent him to Kansas when he recovered. He liked to joke about being in the navy in Kansas.

Ray died in 1997. Even with all the other stuff going through my mind at the time, I was very aware of what was going on when they handed me the American flag that was on his casket. I had a tremendous sense of pride when they gave me the flag and said those words, "On behalf of the president of the United States and a grateful nation." That flag means a great deal to me. I have it in a display box where I can see it every day. It's like looking at a picture of him.

The flag represents your country, and to serve your country is important. You can't do anything to hurt the flag. I don't understand how some people can think it's just a piece of cloth and it doesn't mean anything.

Edward Clark, Captain, USN (Ret.), was born in July 1938 in Girardsville, Pennsylvania, in that state's eastern coal region. He attended the United States Naval Academy, but not in the typical manner. In April 1965, he was a submariner when he answered an urgent request for volunteers to go to Vietnam as advisors to the Vietnamese Navy, which consisted of nothing more than wooden junks. For multiple encounters with the enemy under heavy fire and a job well done, Clark was awarded the Bronze Star for valor, the first American submariner so honored since World War II. Today Clark lives in Alexandria, Virginia.

I was number one academically in my small high school, where I was taught by nuns of the Immaculate Heart of Mary. My mother died when I was a senior and I know she had been very worried about my future. When I graduated, my Dad said to me, "We have no money. I don't know how to counsel you." Even if I'd gotten some kind of scholarship, I couldn't have gone to college because I didn't have any clothes really, or money.

In our house we had a boarder—an older, single guy

named Joe Connor. His nephew went to the Naval Academy, and I went down with Joe to visit the weekend his nephew was graduating. The Naval Academy was a great school, and it was free if you could get in. We didn't have any political clout to get a congressional or senate appointment, so I joined the navy as an enlisted guy because I knew once I was in I could take a test to get into the Naval Academy Preparatory School. I went through boot camp and my four year enlistment as a sailor, but my goal was not to be a sailor, it was to go to the academy. At the appointed hour I showed up at the mess hall to take the test. I got into the prep school. The next year I took a standardized test with about 15,000 other guys—including the congressional appointees—to get into the academy. They just rank ordered you based on the results, and they took about 1,500 guys and I was one of them. So I went to the academy more out of desperation than anything else.

Although I went there for reasons that were not altruistic, once I got there my motivation changed; that's when I first started to understand duty and responsibility and service to your country, and that there was something more valuable than yourself.

When all ships got a message about volunteers for Vietnam, I asked to go. I always thought that if you went to the academy you went to prepare to defend the United States. To me, it was an opportunity for some payback to the country—it was saying we need you to go and that's what I had trained to do.

The flag to me is nothing but a symbol, but it's the symbol of a wonderful thing. I have a deep sense of commitment to the country, so it was always more about the country than the flag for me. I made the transition from symbolism to reality, so I didn't need a flag. When everyone was popping stuff on their cars after September 11, I didn't do that, I didn't think it was necessary. And I don't think you do that because something happens; either do it every day or don't do it at all. I've lived a life of service to the country, I don't need to run around with a flag to tell everyone that, or that I support the country. It's okay that people do it, I don't mind it. Personally, I don't need to. And I didn't.

Harry A. Dooley, Lt. Col. in the U.S. Army reserves, was born in the Port Richmond section of Philadelphia in January 1922. During World War II, he was a navigator on a B-17 in the legendary 91st Bombardment Group of the Eighth Air Force, out of Bassingbourn, England. His brother, James, an infantryman, was killed at Saint-Lo, France. Today, Harry Dooley lives on the same street on which he was born, in Philadelphia.

When I was in grade school, they'd blow the whistles in town at 11:00 A.M. on Armistice Day, and we would all pray to remember the men who died in World War I. I remember, too, that there was a lot of excitement in our neighborhood when Al Smith was running for president in 1928, because he was Irish-Catholic and so were many of us in Port Richmond. They'd have these big parades with people waving flags and stuff, that always ended with a big bonfire in the middle of Lehigh Street. There was some animosity toward the government during the depression, particularly after MacArthur fired on the Bonus Marchers in Washington. That didn't strike people as being patriotic; it just added injury to the insult people already felt being jobless. They had turned against the veterans.

I was unusual for a teenage boy in that I read the paper every day, all the way through. I knew what was going on in the world, and I remember reading about Chamberlain coming back from meeting Hitler in Munich in 1938. I volunteered for the Army Air Corps in 1942. Frankly, I wanted to be an officer because they got the highest pay. These were intelligent guys. If Congress was going to make you an officer, you'd better look the part. We were the cream of the crop. I was always the smartest guy in my high school but, when I got thrown in with these other competitive guys, geez, they were geniuses. The level of desire was unbelievable.

I washed out as a pilot. I got sick the first time I went up in a plane, as did a lot of other guys. There was no such thing as frequent fliers in 1942. They expected me to fly this giant bomber and I didn't even have a driver's license. But they thought I was smart, so they sent me to navigation school.

I got to be a squadron navigator, and when our squadron would lead the group we always had two navigators on board in case one got killed, because 35 other planes were following us. On two missions, my group led the entire Eighth Air Force in a maximum effort over Berlin. There were a thousand planes behind us. Imagine making a wrong turn one of those days! Of course, the Germans knew the lead plane was important and it really was the most dangerous one to be in. That's why we got a three-day pass after each mission and had five missions knocked off our tour of duty. My plane led the first low-level mission over Germany at 12,000 feet, as opposed to the normal 25,000 or so feet. When you're flying that low over a big city, there's a lot of steel coming up at you. They had the Movietone news cameras there when we got back from that one.

Toward the end of the war, we were visiting total devastation on the German cities. It was the only way to break the will of the people. If you got shot down, all you had was your .45 [pistol], and we used to say if that happened you might as well blow your own brains out, because if some farmer finds you and you've just killed his mother, he's going stick a pitchfork right through your belly. They would be filled with rage. For that very reason, they gave us small American flags to put in one of the zippered pockets of our flight suits. If you thought you might be in friendly territory but weren't sure because of the language barrier, you'd show them the flag, and they'd understand you weren't Russian or English. That flag was your universal I.D. There aren't too many people that don't recognize the American flag.

Vincent Laurich was born in Philadelphia in August 1944. His father was a boilermaker on the U.S.S. Boise *when it was torpedoed by the Japanese in the Pacific. The rest of the convoy left the* Boise *for dead, but her men fought on in the Battle of San Sebastian. Vulnerable and disabled, the* Boise *took out five Japanese ships and limped back to Pearl Harbor. The ship sailed to the Philadelphia Navy Yard for repairs, where Vince Laurich, Sr., met his future wife. Vince, Jr., was drafted in 1966, and served in Vietnam with the First Air Cavalry, including its operation to relieve the surrounded marines at Khe Sanh, one of the largest combat assaults in military history. He was severely wounded after four months in country. Today he lives in Prospectville, Pennsylvania, where his Purple Heart and other medals hang on*

a wall in his den, where only he can see them and only when
seated at his desk.

Before I got drafted I was going to school at Temple
[University]. I was a lousy student—I flunked out—but I was
a great dart player. I tested well when I got drafted and went
to OCS [Officer Candidate School] and then I volunteered
to go to ranger school. I knew I was going to Vietnam as a
platoon leader and I figured I may as well be as well trained
as possible. I went over in February 1968. I was a replace-
ment for a lieutenant who was killed in the Tet Offensive.

When you're out in the bush with 120 guys or so, you set
up a perimeter and have a base in a manner of speaking, but
we'd only stay in one spot for a day. We didn't haul flags
around with us and put them up when we set up a perimeter.
That would just tell the bad guys where you were. In the First
Cav and units like the 101st Airborne, you were designed to
be in the field. We didn't have any sense of permanence.
Some guys had tiny little flags they'd stick on top of their de-
fensive position; some guys had the flag on their Zippo
lighter; some guys would paint the flag on their helmet cover
and write stuff like, "I'm from Brooklyn" or "F___ the NVA."

In my mind, I don't know that there's a direct connection
between the soldier and the flag itself. What it symbolizes,
yes, soldiers connect to that. It's the spirit of the flag that's
the thing, and you don't need to see the flag to feel that.

I got shot twice in June 1968, and I was in a body cast
from June until November. I went back to Temple in 1970.
I'd been thrown out for bad grades before the war, so I went
up to see the dean with my cane and played it up a little, told

him I was a war veteran and I was trying to get my act together. He buzzed in his secretary and said, "Put this young man on the rolls." Then he looked at me and said, "If you don't cut it, your ass is going to be back on Broad Street [the main street through the campus]."

It was very difficult going back to college at the time after being in the protected environment of the hospital and my circle of friends. In 1970, you had the SDS [Students for a Democratic Society] and the Vietnam Veterans Against the War, which was a difficult concept for me to grasp. The students were a lot more liberal than I was; they were eighteen and nineteen and I was twenty-six, and what did they know except what they read in the paper? So, it was a tough adjustment. One day I was driving home and I was so pissed off I swore to myself I wouldn't go back. This was a time where if you talked about being a veteran, people thought you were a bad guy. So the vets, we just sort of withdrew. You just didn't tell anyone you were a vet, you know, you didn't announce it at cocktail parties.

In 1975, I had been back in the states for seven years. I had graduated from Temple and was working. My boss at the time was an Indian hobbyist—sort of like a Civil War reenactment kind of thing, but with American Indians as the theme. The group gets together a few times a year and has a powwow. One Friday at work he told me they were getting together the next day, and that I should come. So, I went with my son and daughter, and a friend who wasn't a vet. It was about 8:00 A.M. and they opened up the powwow with a warrior dance of some kind, and it was tied into the raising of the American flag. When it was time to raise the flag, they said only a warrior could raise the flag, and my boss motioned to me to come out and raise the flag. It was really my first public acknowledgment as a warrior. It took this bridge from an ancient culture to make me feel like I wasn't hiding anymore.

Whitney Smith was born in Lexington, Massachusetts, in 1940. He first became interested in the American flag when his father brought one from World War II home for him.

I've quite honestly always been a contrarian, and I have a very cerebral relationship with the flag. I have taken the vocational calling of vexillology to mean that I have to be like a Martian, and I've dropped amidst these people running around with these sticks and pieces of cloth and I say, "Whoa, what's going on here. I need to find out." And I learn a lot by posing unpopular questions or ones that no one's asked before. . . . What if?

I also feel strongly that the freedom that is the essence of this country to pursue our dream, whatever that may be, is a rare and precious commodity. And I don't mean worldwide, I mean in the United States. It's under constant challenge. Every day you turn around and there's someone who wants to put us back in the Middle Ages. And I've always instinctively been supportive of minorities. If this country means what it says, we have to stop pretending that it's rich white males that count—black people are human beings, gay people are human beings, atheists are human beings—and the flag to me means that. And that puts the obligation on me to work to defend that. And it is tricky, because I want to be a scholar and be objective, but I do have very strong feelings. So in terms of pride of country, I'm very cerebral.

I never served in the armed forces. I've never been in the government. I've never been a joiner. I don't fly a flag on a regular basis. But I don't feel that's the essence of the flag. The flag is the outward expression of our life. It's my thoughts and actions that count, not the way I look.

ON JULY 20, 1969, astronauts Neil Armstrong and Buzz Aldrin jumped out of their lunar lander and onto the surface of the moon. They planted an American flag that required a wire frame to keep it outstretched in the gravity-free atmosphere.

Exactly seven years later, in 1976—the American Bicentennial—at 4:53 A.M. PDT, the Viking 1 unmanned space craft landed on the surface of Mars. Painted on the side of Viking 1 was the American flag of thirteen stripes, alternate red and white, and a union of fifty blue stars. The landing was within six days of being precisely 199 years from the day the Congress resolved the flag of the thirteen United States would represent a new constellation. If those men of the Marine Committee in Philadelphia in 1777 could only know how perfectly they had chosen their words.

IN THE EARLY MONTHS OF 2002, some people began to wonder whether it was okay to take their American flags in from the porch and from their cars. Uneasy questions arose that the flag can produce: "If I take it down after putting it up in a surge of patriotism, am I less of a patriot once I put it back in the closet? What will the neighbors think?" In a na-

A New Constellation: Buzz Aldrin stands beside the Stars and Stripes during the *Apollo 11* mission.

tion that prides itself on self-determination, we can be oddly obsessed with what other people think of even the simplest individual acts. As such, we often attempt to impose black-and-white clarity upon issues that clearly resist it.

There is no correlation between individual patriotism and the display of the Stars and Stripes. The flag is not required to define a person's sense of place in the American family; many people use it for this purpose, however, and, in so doing, create a vivid picture of the flag's true spirit. The flag flies from pickup trucks, Harley-Davidsons and SUVs; it hangs on barns and diners and corporate headquarters; it appears on athletic uniforms, NBA backboards and T-shirts worn by teenage girls; it decorates the hard hats of pile drivers and ironworkers; and is pinned to the breast of bespoke tailored suits. Driving from Bucks County, Pennsylvania, to Boston in February 2002, I counted more than five hundred flags before giving up counting on the outskirts of Boston. One of those flags was stuck in the top of a tall fir tree in northern New York, along the Taconic Parkway. There wasn't a residence or commercial building within miles. Whoever placed the flag in the tree went to a great deal of effort, and it told an anonymous story: "I am American."

The flag tells that same story in a thousand different ways every day, revealing the good, the bad, and the ugly of the American character. We are jingoistic and crass, not above exploiting and warping love of country in the name of television ratings, commerce, and easy, hollow political sentiment. We are greedy and hypocritical, and all too willingly swayed by those who love the flag, but are unwilling to accept that it need not mean the same thing to everyone. *And,* we are brave and we know it, no matter what the people of other nations think. We are ambitious and free, willing to shoulder any burden in the name of liberty, either for ourselves, in unison with, or on behalf of, others. We are dreamers and builders, more quixotic, more questing, than any nation in the history of the world.

Whatever America has been, is, and will be, is based on countless individual acts and beliefs. The American flag represents every one of them.

BIBLIOGRAPHY

Garrison, Webb. *Civil War Curiosities: Strange Stories, Oddities, Events and Coincidences.* Nashville, Tennessee: Rutledge Hill Press, 1994

Goldstein, Robert Justin. *Desecrating the American Flag: Key Documents of the Controversy from the Civil War to 1995.* Syracuse, New York: Syracuse University Press, 1996

Furlong, William Rea and Byron McCandless. *So Proudly We Hail: The History of the United States Flag.* Washington, D.C.: Smithsonian Institution Press, 1981

Libby, Frederick. *Horses Don't Fly: A Memoir of World War I.* New York: Arcade Publishing, 2000

Marvin, Carolyn and David W. Ingles. *Blood Sacrifice and the Nation: Totem Rituals and the American Flag.* Cambridge, England: Cambridge University Press, 1999

Preble, George Henry. *Origin and History of the American Flag (Vols. I and II).* Philadelphia: Nicholas L. Brown, 1917

Smith, Whitney. *Long May It Wave! The National Flag of the United States Past, Present and Future.* Winchester, Massachusetts: Flag Research Center, 1998

———. *The Flag Bulletin (Vol. XIX, No. 2, Vol. XXXVIII, No. 2, Vol. XXXIX. No. 1).* Winchester, Massachusetts: The Flag Research Center (1980, 1999, 2000)

INDEX

Page numbers in *italics* refer to illustrations.

ABOUT THE AUTHOR

*M*ichael Corcoran is a writer and editor whose multimedia experience includes magazines, books, radio, and video. He was editor-in-chief of *Golf Illustrated,* and managing editor of ABC Sports/Jack Nicklaus Productions' *The Wide World of Golf* video series. Corcoran has written for and edited *Golf Digest* and *Men's Health.* He is author or co-author of eight books, including *Duel in the Sun* (Simon & Schuster, 2002), and teaches at Temple University in Philadelphia. He lives in Springtown, Pennsylvania, with his wife and three children.